DATA ANALYSIS FOR PSYCHOLOGY

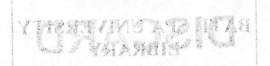

DATA ANALYSIS FOR PSYCHOLOGY

George Dunbar

Lecturer in Psychology
University of Warwick

A member of the Hodder Headline Group
LONDON • SYDNEY • AUCKLAND

First published in Great Britain in 1998 by
Arnold, a member of the Hodder Headline Group,
338 Euston Road, London NW1 3BH
175 Fifth Avenue, New York, NY 10010

Distributed exclusively in the USA by
St Martin's Press, Inc.
175 Fifth Avenue, New York, NY 10010

British Library Cataloguing in Publication Data
A catalogue record for this book is available from the British Library

Library of Congress Cataloging-in-Publication Data
A catalog record for this book is available from the Library of Congress

ISBN 0 340 69133 6 (hb)
ISBN 0 340 69136 0 (pb)

Publisher: Naomi Meredith
Production Editor: James Rabson
Production Controller: Sarah Kett
Cover designer: Julie Martin

Typeset in 10/12 Palatino by Photoprint, Torquay, Devon.
Printed and bound in Great Britain by J W Arrowsmith Ltd, Bristol

To Romy

CONTENTS

PREFACE

This book is aimed between introductory texts and advanced texts. My purpose is to provide a conceptual framework that allows students and researchers to understand the data analysis process and to get more out of their data. Once this conceptual framework is grasped, advanced texts become more accessible, and I hope that readers will go on to consult many of these texts listed in the references. The emphasis is on conceptual understanding and I have occasionally simplified the presentation of concepts to maintain that focus. In one or two cases, this means that I say things that a statistician would wish to qualify. For example, I explain analysis of covariance in terms of an analysis of variance of residuals. That is not strictly true, I know, but it is very close to the truth and, indeed, a convenient fiction. My purpose, then, is to develop the reader's understanding rather than to present a definitive treatise on statistics. Because I am a psychologist and not a statistician, my emphasis is on data analysis rather than statistical theory.

This is designed as an intermediate text, and so I have assumed that readers will have already taken an introductory course in statistics of some kind, and that they will have covered topics including significance testing and the analysis of variance. I have also assumed that when you analyse your own data, you will have access to a computer software package for statistics, although the book is not geared to any particular package. All the figures and data analyses presented were prepared using Systat (Wilkinson, 1986).

The influence of Tukey's work will be clear. I would also like to acknowledge the help I have received from many people. My family have continued to provide unquestioning support and warmth that I scarcely deserve. Four anonymous reviewers made helpful suggestions. Mary-Ann Hill of Systat Inc. was kind enough to send me a copy of her book (Hill, 1990) which helped greatly when I was beginning to use that package, Glyn Collis has answered many questions, Martin Skinner helped me track down some references at a vital moment, and Greg Jones first suggested I write this, although Naomi Meredith of Arnold succeeded in actually getting me to do it. Messrs Flett and Guthrie bear some responsibility for anything that is good in this, and many students over the last few years have contributed to reducing the amount that is bad. Errors or confusions that remain are not their responsibility.

George Dunbar

1 INTRODUCTION: DATA ANALYSIS

This text is intended for psychology students taking a second course in research methods. I expect you will have looked at topics like significance testing or descriptive statistics before, and that you will have encountered tests like analysis of variance (ANOVA) at some point. This book focuses on putting data analysis to use in the context of a research program. It eschews detailed mathematical explanations or inspection of detailed statistical calculation. Rather than concentrating on tests, we emphasize understanding the data. On the other hand, the book is not simply about the logic of experimental method. Instead, it concentrates on the development of a systematic approach to data analysis. The approach is based on what statisticians call the general linear model, with liberal doses of exploratory data analysis. The general linear model provides a family of techniques for testing relationships among variables, establishing their strength and significance. Exploratory data analysis is an approach aimed at making patterns in data easy to visualize. This book considers data analysis as a framework of methods, and emphasizes the integration of different techniques in the analysis of a data set.

The material is presented verbally rather than algebraically. This will come as a relief to some readers, but may raise the hackles of others. Normally, nowadays, statistical work is carried out using computer software and, indeed, many of the techniques described would be impractical to carry out by hand. This means that the direct use of formulae often does not arise in practice. Moreover, the raw score formulae for many statistics are not edifying. Calculating the statistics manually may not teach you that much. I believe this is especially true in the early stages of learning about data analysis. There is a large range of techniques to cover, and time spent unravelling formulae or mathematical derivations can be a distraction. Better to gain a strategic grasp of what is available and how it fits into the problem solving environment of a research project. I will therefore assume that you have access to computer software for calculation.

Although you will not be bashed on the head with formulae, you do, however, need to understand something of the rationale underlying major techniques. The rationale underlying a technique is its conceptual foundation. The reason for exploring the rationale behind methods is that it is not enough to work with a fixed list of techniques that you can apply. You need to understand enough that you can flexibly apply techniques to new data sets. Practically every data set is different. Every experiment generates something unexpected. Only if you understand the basis of methods can you learn how to adapt your stock of techniques to new data sets. You will also find that the better you understand the rationale underlying a technique, the easier it is to make good use of advanced textbooks that can guide you when you come across new data analysis problems.

Many students of psychology do have good backgrounds in mathematics, and find the omission of derivations frustrating. If you are such a person and find the absence of mathematical detail frustrating, you will find a more detailed set of explanations available in the advanced references listed. This text emphasizes a strategic view of the data analysis process, and the relationship between data analysis and theory in psychology.

Always, the purpose of data analysis is to assist the psychologist to understand some aspect of human behaviour. Psychologists produce hypotheses, opinions, conjectures, ideas — even theories. All these things are useful because they explain some psychological phenomenon or other. As people trying to understand human behaviour, we need explanations of that behaviour. Explanation helps us understand behaviour in terms of causes. However, because we claim to be scientific, at least insofar as we study human behaviour, we need to test these explanations. This is done by observing and measuring patterns of behaviour. Many kinds of behaviour can be observed, many kinds of measurement can be taken. And people can be studied in different kinds of situation — some natural, some artificial. We need to be sure that:

- the methods we use to obtain measurements are clean (data hygiene);
- the methods we use to evaluate measurements are sound (data analysis).

For example, if you use a questionnaire you will want to establish that it is reliable. If you collect reaction times, you will check that the clock works. When you observe behaviour, you do not intrude upon the behavioural setting. These are matters of data hygiene. The data you take away from the events you study must reflect those events accurately. The process of gathering data must not influence the events themselves. Once the data is gathered, its key features must be identified. If the scores of one group are consistently higher than those of another group, you need to be able to detect and measure this difference. If subjects respond more quickly in one condition than another, again you need methods that will reveal this pattern and give you a precise indication of its importance.

Cutting through the jungle of numbers to the underlying structure is the business of data analysis.

These points are central to the process of investigation. They go to the heart of empirical psychology, and they are what this text is about, the problem of evidential soundness in psychological research: how can we get good data to evaluate our explanations?

Here are some key topics we will cover.

- How to explore a data set and test hypotheses about the data set;
- what a statistical model is;
- how statistical models relate to hypothesis testing;
- the purpose of exploratory data analysis.

So, by the end of the book, you will be able to analyse a data set and you will be able to explain key concepts like statistical model, error, or exploratory data analysis.

1.1   SIMPLE HYPOTHESIS TESTING

Data analysis can be done relatively simply, and it will be useful to describe briefly the conventional approach to this that is frequently taught and with which you may already be familiar. Later, I will build on this basic framework. We can use a designed experiment example to show the typical stages of data analysis. Although we focus on a designed experiment, the same general principles apply to data analysis in other contexts.

An experiment is carried out to test the effectiveness of three pain-relieving drugs. Three groups of patients are each given one of the drugs. There are ten participants in each group. The experimenter records the amount of time, in seconds, that subjects can withstand a painful stimulus. (Ouch!) Data analysis proceeds in three conventional stages. First, a test is chosen. Second, its result is computed. Finally, the outcome is assessed and reported.

1.1.1 Choose a test

To choose a test you work out what kind of assessment you want to make, formulate an explicit hypothesis and select a test, perhaps using a decision chart. Ideally, you do this before running the experiment to avoid the risk of waking up one morning with unanalysable data and an imminent deadline. In our example, we want to compare the means (μ) of more than two groups. A typical chart tells us to use a one-way ANOVA. An alpha (α) level is chosen and the hypothesis (H) is expressed formally:

Let $\alpha = 0.05$

$H_0: \mu_1 = \mu_2 = \mu_3$ (no effect attributable to the difference between groups)

H_1: 'At least one of the group means is different'

1.1.2 Do the calculation that the chosen test demands

For a one-way ANOVA, you compare the differences between the three groups to the variation among individuals within each group.

    (i) $MS_{between} = SS_{between} \div df_{between}$
    (ii) $MS_{within} = SS_{within} \div df_{within}$

Here, MS is the 'mean square' which indicates how much scores vary. There is one MS for scores between groups, and one for scores within. If the groups have equal pain tolerance (the drugs have identical effects) then you expect the two mean squares to be equal (there is no more difference between people taking different drugs than there is among people taking the same drug). If they are equal, then their ratio will be 1. The *F*-ratio is calculated to see what their ratio in fact is.

    (iii) $F = MS_{between} \div MS_{within}$

The detailed calculation of the sums of squared deviations (SS) is not detailed here. However, do note that two separate degrees of freedom (df) values are involved: df_{within} and $df_{between}$. The $df_{between}$ is related to the number of conditions being compared. The df_{within} usually relates to the number of subjects. You must always report both these degrees of freedom when describing the results of an ANOVA.

1.1.3 Report the result

With df = 2, 8 values of *F* that exceed 4.07 are so rare they will occur by chance alone fewer than five times in 100. If the obtained value exceeds this critical value we are entitled to conclude that there is a significant treatment effect.

In practice, you would then go on to make comparisons between the means of individual drugs to identify the locus of the obtained effect. These three stages comprise the basic conventional model of data analysis, and they constitute a minimum adequate procedure. The data analysis template given in section 1.4 builds on this conventional model and indicates some additional features of high quality data analysis. The rest of the book serves to elaborate this template with specific examples and techniques.

1.2   DATA ANALYSIS AND RESEARCH

You must go beyond this conventional simple hypothesis testing not because it is in any sense incorrect, but because it is too narrow. Data analysis cannot be done mechanically, guided only by a flow chart, ending with a snapshot from a single test. Real data from real subjects is incredibly rich. It carries traces of the real psychological mechanisms generating behaviour. To reveal these underlying processes demands an intelligent and creative element to data analysis. You need to sift through the numbers looking not simply for confirmation (or, strictly speaking, disconfirmation) of your initial hypothesis. Of course you want to check out your initial thoughts, but sometimes the reality unveiled by your study is more complex than you anticipated when you initially framed it. For many reasons, few studies in psychology conform to the ideal model of simple hypothesis testing, although the way we write papers sometimes suggests that they do.

First, of course, research comes in different forms. These range in 'purity' from iterative experimentation to observational studies. In iterative experimentation, a sequence of hypotheses is tested in successive experiments. For example, experiment 1 tests whether high frequency words are recognized more quickly than low frequency words. If not, then perhaps we conclude that frequency is irrelevant to word recognition. If there is a difference, then experiment 2 is conducted to satisfy the doubts of a sceptic who could argue that experiment 1 confounds frequency with, say, imageability. In this experiment, the high and low frequency words are matched so that they are equally imageable. Each experiment is motivated by specific possible beliefs or explanations for observed data, and is designed to test those beliefs. Successive experiments are designed to exclude competing hypotheses and to focus on a particular explanation. The converse of this is an entirely observational study. For example, a psychologist interested in the social behaviour of infants might initiate their research by simply watching children and observing what occurs. The observer is prepared to record any behaviour that seems interesting. No preconceptions exist about which behaviours will count as interesting. This kind of investigation does not test hypotheses. Rather, it serves to accumulate and systematize experience that can be used to formulate hypotheses, hypotheses that can be tested later, another time. Conventional data analysis is in a sense idealistic: it idealizes the concept of research by treating it as hypothesis tesing. Most real research requires a combination of hypothesis testing and observation.

Not all research fits the ideal experimental model that conventional data analysis squeezes it into. Sometimes research fails to match up because psychology is young and it is not clear what a good hypothesis would be, or our hypotheses are tentative: we cannot be certain we are asking the right questions. When an area is relatively new, many researchers will rely on observation to build up their understanding of the phenomena of interest. Furthermore, there can be a trade-off between 'ideal' experimentation and ecological validity. In order to test a specific hypothesis in an experiment, you need to control aspects of the situation that might influence behaviour but which are not relevant to the hypothesis. As you do this, of course, you change the behavioural setting and so you run the risk of changing the behaviour. A researcher may, therefore, choose to stand back from a phenomenon if intrusion might distort naturally occuring behaviour. Indeed, many psychologists now believe that some phenomena observed under controlled, experimental conditions in the laboratory do not occur in everyday behaviour. Even when it is possible to frame an experimental hypothesis and set up a controlled experiment, we still need to examine the data carefully. Sometimes unexpected things occur, or a variable that was not controlled turns out to influence behaviour. Simple hypothesis testing can fail to reveal results of this kind. We need data analysis skills that allow data to speak to us despite our expectations. Conventional data analysis contributes to this, but we can go further.

1.3 DATA, MODELS AND ERROR

In the next two sections, we map out the essentials of the approach to statistical testing emphasized in this text. Very briefly, it goes like this. You run a study and collect some data. To understand the results, you build a model and test whether it fits the data well. That's it. In the sections that follow, I will develop and explain this idea a little more.

The statistical model you build is created in order to account for the data. For each data point you can partly explain why it came to be the number it is: this is your model of why things are the way they are. If data points are all identical, the model can be very simple at the statistical level ($x = $ constant, where x stands for each measurement or score). For real data, they are not all the same. Your task is to explain how each data point has come to be the way it is. Why did a subject do better on one occasion than another? For example, you run an experiment in which you flash a number on the screen, and the subject has to type [y] if it is odd, [n] if it's even. Over 10 attempts, you get the following RTs (response times) in milliseconds (ms):

Subject A — [293 293 293 293 293 293 293 293 293 293]
Subject B — [346 412 403 418 374 352 396 422 388 379]

How do you explain that variation in subject B's scores? Why are they not all the same? What kinds of things can affect subject B's perform-ance? What is the effect of these factors? These questions can be addressed by building a statistical model.
1) A very simple, trivial, model can be built for subject A, M1.1.

M1.1: RT = constant

M1.1: RT = 293

This 'model' represents the behaviour of subject A. It says that subject A responds with the same latency on each trial. Subject A is probably not a person. The most basic model that can be used for subject B's data is also simple.

M1.2: RT = constant + (random) error

M1.2: RT = 389 + error

That is, each RT comes to be what it is because it has two parts, one part due to a constant time built in by the nature of the task; the other just random variation in the time a person takes to perform because: a cloud passes by the window of the room; they get distracted; or their finger slips. This model is still not very interesting from the point of view of theory construction in psychology. It does not go much further than M1.1 in identifying relevant factors. All it really says is 'subject B is just like subject A (the robot) except that B is noisier.' In other words, people are just robots that make random errors during processing (sorry, thinking . . .).
    It is all very well writing down equations like this, but it's not much help unless we can attach some meaning to the terms in the equation. For example, what is the constant? How much is the error? This is what statistical techniques like ANOVA and so on are designed to provide: the numerical interpretation of the model. They give us a means of testing our model of the data against the data itself. Essentially all statistics work in the same way. Each statistic embodies a template of the way data would look if it exactly matched a model. It compares the real data obtained in your experiment with its own theoretical model and gives you precise, numerical information about the fit of the model to the data.
    We calculated the constant in M1.2 simply by taking the mean of all the data points. This is called fitting the model to the data. (This is actually also what we did for subject A — 293 was the mean of A's reaction times.) The mean of subject B's reaction times (RTs) is 389 ms. So our model becomes:

M1.2 RT = 389 + error

In other words, each particular reaction time is composed by adding a random error to 389. For instance, the first RT was:

346 = 389 + (− 53)

For some unexplained reason (a surge of caffeine tickling the neuro-transmitters perhaps?) the subject shaved about 1/20th of a second off her 'standard' RT on this occasion. On the next occasion:

412 = 389 + 23

Some random source of variation added 23 ms to the RT actually taken by the subject. With M1.2 it is very easy to attach numbers to the components in the model, and we do not need any fancy techniques. This example is easy from the point of view of calculation. Bear in mind that analyses involving more complex calculations are nevertheless based on a similar concept. You identify a model, you match it up to the data and use statistical calculations to associate terms in the model with numerical values, and you assess the significance of these numerical values. These operations correspond roughly to the three steps of conventional data analysis we mentioned above. In the first step, you construct a model, where in conventional data analysis you choose a statistic. You then fit the model to the data, which corresponds to doing the calculation. Third, you assess the statistical significance of the result, just as you do in conventional data analysis.

Although the model M1.2 is extremely, not to say excruciatingly, simple, we can use it to make four important points about statistical modelling. These concepts will be developed in later chapters. On a first reading you might want to just skim them.

1. First, each score is broken down into two parts by this approach. In M1.2, these parts are the constant and the residual. More generally, we would call these parts explained variance and error variance.
2. Second, gathering the residuals for data points lets you look at the overall error for the dataset. This overall term, called the error mean square (MS_{error}), can be used to construct tests that tell us whether a result is significant or not. Significance testing works in general by comparing the variance explained in a model to the error variance.
3. The residual error for any individual data point (e.g. subject B's first response has a residual of − 48 ms) is a combination of several — perhaps very many — unidentified effects. For example, on this occasion perhaps a bus passes by the laboratory window, distracting the subject and adding 100 ms to the RT, but the stimulus is familiar, perhaps repeated from a previous list, cutting 148 ms from the time.

Thus the residual error could be made up of two effects which partially cancel each other out.

$$346 = 394 + (100 - 148)$$

4. Sources of error may lie not just in the subject, though subjects are an important source of error variance, especially in psychology experiments. Other sources of error include your apparatus and you, the experimenter. We can therefore differentiate, for example, measurement error from error in general. Error in measurement is just one part of statistical error.

In general, so-called parametric tests, like ANOVA, make assumptions about the pattern of error you can get. For example, ANOVA assumes that the residuals represent the effect of random error. The residuals are therefore expected to be normally distributed with a mean of zero. In other words, we expect errors to occur by chance, and to increase measurements as often as they decrease them. This is an assumption made about the distribution of errors. In Chapter 3 we will look at the assumptions of various statistics and review the ways you can test them, and what you should do if they are not met.

The following point is important, though slightly tricky to grasp at first. The word error has a technical meaning in this context. What counts as error from the point of view of a statistical model is just everything that is not part of the rest of the model. In M1.1, there is no error, statistically. In M1.2, everything apart from the constant effect 'mean time to make a response' is error. However, you can move things out of the error component into the body of the model. This is the guts of research and data analysis really. Call it taking control of error. In M1.2, error is everything that contributes to variation in scores from one attempt to the next. However, you can move specific sources of variance from error into explicit components of the model. For example, another source of error may well be that the subject, on average, finds it easier to identify even numbers as even numbers than she finds it classifying odd numbers: it may just be easier to spot an even number. That is, there may be a systematic difference in RTs that we can attribute to the category the target number came from. If we do this, we get a third possible model for our data, M1.3.

M1.3: RT = constant + category + error

In other words, we predict that each observed data value, each RT, is produced by, or made out of, three components. The first is a constant effect attributable to the general task of responding to numbers. The second is a systematic component of variance, due to differences between odd and even numbers. And the third part consists of just whatever is left over. This is all variance in scores that cannot be accounted for by the grand mean and the effect of category. It is the residual or error variance.

In subsequent chapters, I will not usually write the constant in model statements. This is just to simplify the presentation. For all the models in this book, however, you can assume that a constant term is part of the model.

We now need to distinguish between random error and systematic error. In M1.2, error has two components: it includes both random error and systematic error attributable to the category of the target number. In experimental work we aim to control all sources of systematic error either by eliminating them (e.g. only ever using even numbers as stimuli, and then sticking to the simpler model, M1.2) or by explicitly introducing them as factors in the design (i.e. have separate conditions for odd and even numbers and use the model M1.3 instead). The model for the one-way ANOVA example we looked at earlier is shown in M1.4. Recall that this study looked at how long participants who had been given different pain-killing drugs could withstand pain.

M1.4: PainTime = constant + drug + error

Table 1.1 displays some data for three fictitious participants which we can use to illustrate the way a model like this splits each score into parts.

The constant is again calculated to be the overall mean, which for these scores is 3. There were separate groups for each drug. Take for instance drug B: the mean for this group was 4. We therefore attribute an effect of +1 to drug B because the average score for someone taking this drug is 1 more than the average overall. We can, then, use M1.4 to describe the final observation in the group given drug B as:

$$PainTime(B,3) = constant + effect\ of\ drug\ B + residual$$
$$5 \qquad\quad = 3 \qquad\quad +1 \qquad\qquad\qquad +1$$

The mean for drug C is 6, and so its effect is said to be $(6 - constant) = 3$:

$$PainTime(C,3) = constant + effect\ of\ drug\ C + residual$$
$$5 \qquad\quad = 3 \qquad\quad +3 \qquad\qquad\qquad -1$$

Generally speaking, we are interested in the relationships between groups of observations. This is what ANOVA tests: is there an overall

Table 1.1 Time pain was endured

Drug A	Drug B	Drug C
3	4	7
1	3	6
2	5	5

difference in the means of observations in different groups? Is the effect of using different drugs statistically significant? Model fitting is not essentially different from hypothesis testing. Rather, it is a different way of looking at hypothesis testing. It is useful to look at it this way because:

- it emphasizes the way we partition variance into components attributable to different sources;
- it provides a foundation of concepts with which a range of statistical techniques can be described and explained.

We can also see from this simple example that as well as asking whether the effects of drugs differ significantly, we can ask questions about the magnitude of these effects. Here, drug C had a larger effect than drug B. This is important when assessing the practical importance of findings.

1.4   DATA ANALYSIS TEMPLATE

To end this chapter, here is an outline of the stages of data analysis that will be amplified subsequently. I have stressed that conventional data analysis is expanded in practice, and supported by a careful examination of the data. The template here represents a sequence of steps to follow, and these steps apply to many kinds of study.

1. Exploratory data analysis
2. Data repair
3. Construct model and test significance
4. Exploratory data analysis revisited: check residuals
5. Carry out planned comparisons and estimate effects
6. Make unplanned tests *post hoc*

The details of this template are not important at this stage — they will be developed later. However, you should note the extra steps both before and after the conventional test of significance. In the approach we will develop, simple hypothesis testing provides the backbone of data analysis, but it is supported by careful and detailed examination of the data. This additional framework addresses particular statistical and practical questions, and sets the process of data analysis realistically in relation to an unfolding project or program of research.

1.5   SUMMARY

Hypothesis testing using significance tests is a key part of data analysis for psychologists. However, it is valuable to build on this with additional techniques that allow you to examine your data set more thoroughly.

The process of building and refining a statistical model provides a foundation for this approach to data analysis. The concept of a statistical model provides a unified framework for understanding a variety of statistical techniques.

2 EXPLORATORY DATA ANALYSIS

John Tukey's magnificent book *Exploratory Data Analysis* appeared in 1977, although the manuscript had circulated previously. It is, I think, one of the most wonderful books I have read. It cuts to the heart of data analysis and places in focus two key ideas. First, data analysis is done for a reason. It is a response to the purposes of science. It exists to allow people to understand and interpret phenomena. It exists to let you see the world. Second, data analysis is a process. To understand data, you need to examine it repeatedly, viewing the results in different ways, refining your understanding of the object of study. This process can involve the evaluation of specific hypotheses, but also admits a search for the unexpected. The data you gather in a study contains information about the phenomenon you have studied. Exploratory data analysis (EDA) emphasizes a search through data to reveal patterns. These patterns contain information which can help you understand the events observed in your study. To understand EDA, we need to cover five basic issues:

- Why is it important to find patterns?
- What counts as a pattern? (i.e. what is a pattern in data?)
- What techniques can we use to find patterns?
- When can such techniques be used?
- How should the results be interpreted?

By going through some specific instances of data analysis, we can start to answer such questions. Tukey (1977) uses examples from the physical sciences to illustrate his points, and I will borrow one of those examples here.

2.1 REVEALING PATTERNS

The first case examined illustrates the basic technical principles of EDA. Raw data is hard to understand. The data analyst needs an alternative way to present the data to herself. A representation that the eye finds congenial is of more practical use than one that is hard to make sense of. Important features of a dataset are sometimes hard to perceive when you just look at a table of the raw data. EDA aims to provide ways of presenting data that make the data easier to understand.

Tukey uses the example of Rayleigh's research. Lord Rayleigh did research in the late 19th century trying to find out how heavy nitrogen is. He did a number of careful experiments, each designed to produce some nitrogen. He started with a chemical compound which includes nitrogen (different compounds in different experiments). He then did something to this compound to isolate a fixed amount of nitrogen. Thus, he used a chemical technique to purify the compound and thereby produce a sample of nitrogen. A fixed volume (say, one litre) of this nitrogen was then weighed, and the weight was recorded. Lord Rayleigh repeated this experiment 15 times, and ended up with 15 estimates of the weight of one standard volume of nitrogen. His results are displayed in Table 2.1

Look at Table 2.1 for a moment or two. The table accurately represents the data. All the information from the study is present in its rows and columns. However, most people do not find that any pattern is immediately discernable. Nevertheless, there is an important regularity in the data. If you examine the numbers very carefully, this pattern may become clear. What Rayleigh found by carefully looking at the data was that there appeared to be two kinds of nitrogen. The two types differ in weight. Tukey (1977) looks at alternative ways of plotting this data. Some of these alternatives make the pattern easy to see, while others obscure it.

Table 2.1   Rayleigh data, adapted from Tukey (1977), original source Lord Rayleigh (1894). 'On an anomaly encountered in determinations of the density of nitrogen gas', *Proceedings of the Royal Society* (London) 55, 340–44.

Date	Source compound	Extraction method	Weight observed
29.11.93	NO	hot iron	2.30143
5.12.93	NO	hot iron	2.29816
6.12.93	NO	hot iron	2.30182
8.12.93	NO	hot iron	2.29890
12.12.93	Air	hot iron	2.31017
14.12.93	Air	hot iron	2.30986
19.12.93	Air	hot iron	2.31010
22.12.93	Air	hot iron	2.31001
26.12.93	N_2O	hot iron	2.29889
28.12.93	N_2O	hot iron	2.29940
9.1.94	NH_4NO_2	hot iron	2.29849
13.1.94	NH_4NO_2	hot iron	2.29889
27.1.94	Air	ferrous hydrate	2.31024
30.1.94	Air	ferrous hydrate	2.31030
1.2.94	Air	ferrous hydrate	2.31028

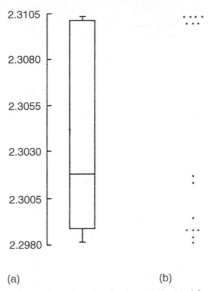

(a)   (b)

Figure 2.1   Alternative plots of the Rayleigh data, adapted from Tukey (1977)

For example, he points out that a box and whisker plot (he actually uses a slightly different type of plot, which he terms a schematic plot) of the data set as a whole tends to mask the pattern (see Fig. 2.1(a)). However, a dot plot of the data makes the separation of two groups very clear (Fig. 2.1(b)). The box and whisker plot reveals a pattern, but does not assist greatly in accounting for it. A further step makes the underlying source of this difference more apparent. If the data are divided into two groups using the identity of the source chemical compound as a grouping variable, then side-by-side box and whisker plots show that there is a regular difference between samples derived from different sources. In fact, further investigation showed that the heavier samples were not pure nitrogen. They contained traces of argon, which is heavier than nitrogen. The argon in the samples derived from air made these samples heavier. As it happened, argon had not been discovered before this, so they had a wee celebration. The work following up on the anomaly noted by Rayleigh led directly to the discovery of a new element.

In this example, the pattern is that the data fall into two separate groups. The technique is simple: find a graph that shows clearly that the distance between the groups is large compared to the distance between points within each group. The point of this example is not to demonstrate that one type of representation is always better than another. Rather, searching for an appropriate way to represent the data is an active process. You may not intially be aware that specific patterns are present. Viewing the data from different perspectives using different methods to represent it can allow you to discover unanticipated regularities. Tukey's example also illustrates another important point. As data

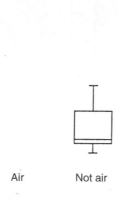

Air   Not air

Figure 2.2 Plot of the Rayleigh data grouped by source, adapted from Tukey (1977)

analysis proceeds, it seeks more refined descriptions of the data. Figure 2.2 goes further than Fig. 2.1(b) because it links the distinction between the two data sets to another variable. In this case, the other variable is the source of the sample.

Tukey also points out that the most appropriate representation can depend on the purpose of the experiment. If the aim is to do basic research on the mass of an element, then like Rayleigh we want a representation that clearly separates the two groups. On the other hand, if we are trying to work out how much to charge an industrialist who wants us to transport large amounts of nitrogen, we are not going to be interested in emphasizing such small differences. Many textbooks argue that graphs should never be constructed that emphasize small differences. The axes of graphs, they say, should be constructed so that, for example, the scale is not truncated to exaggerate a small difference. However, for certain purposes small differences may be important. Graphs and other data representations should be constructed in an appropriate way. They should be drawn to reveal relevant detail.

2.2 INTERPRETING PATTERNS

You will no doubt have had drummed into you that descriptive statistics are not sufficient. Scientific research does not proceed by simple induction: it is not enough to simply observe. And indeed, this is not unreasonable. Psychological science works within a framework of hypothesis testing. Most psychologists, therefore, would not find a simple graphical display convincing or even persuasive. They would demand to see the hypothesis tested using a statistic that comes with a *p*-value. That is, they would ask for further evidence, in the shape of an inferential statistic, that the observed difference is statistically significant. This is important in psychology perhaps especially because the phenomena and the processes psychologists study are noisy. Differences are rarely as clear cut as they can seem to be in the physical sciences.

However, there are one or two points that are worth making about the relationship between descriptive techniques, EDA and inferential statistics. First, in certain situations descriptive methods can allow inferences to be drawn. These are generally cases where a difference is clear cut. For example, Fig. 2.2 in fact demonstrates clearly that the difference is statistically significant. This is because the range of data values from the two sets of samples do not overlap at all. Second, in many instances techniques such as ANOVA or multiple regression, which are usually thought of as inferential techniques, can be viewed as providing a description of the data. These techniques involve the construction of a statistical model of the data. This model accounts for the data in certain terms. This account is given in terms of the predictor variables included in the model. Metaphorically, these predictors are like colours on a palette. They provide the shades in which a picture of the data can be drawn. Thus, there is a degree of overlap between descriptive and inferential techniques. Some descriptive techniques are available that can embody information relevant to inferential judgements, and some inferential techniques can be used to construct models.

An alternative distinction that can be useful is one between exploratory and confirmatory analysis. Exploratory analysis is concerned with finding good descriptions. A good description may be simple, for example, or provocative. Confirmatory analysis, on the other hand, seeks to test a hypothesis. In this book, I will not labour either of these distinctions. Nevertheless, it is useful to reflect in your own data analysis practice on how your analysis fits in with them. Think, as you apply different techniques, about whether what you are doing is really exploratory, or is testing a hypothesis.

The example of Rayleigh's work also illustrates another important point about the interpretation of exploratory techniques. The best use of a pattern discovered by exploratory work is often as the germ of a further experiment. For example, just seeing the distinction between different nitrogen samples was not the end of Rayleigh's project. A great deal of additional work had to be done. This additional research fitted better into the classical hypothesis testing understanding of the scientific process. Exploratory techniques help us to bridge the gap between one experiment and the next. Noticing the pattern was the beginning of a new phase of his research. EDA has an important role as a source of 'suggestions for further research'. EDA raises questions. Contrast this with confirmatory data analysis (hypothesis testing), whose output is a decision. Confirmatory data analysis settles questions, exploratory data analysis raises new questions for investigation. Effective research requires both.

2.3 MULTIPLICITY

Indeed, EDA carries certain risks if too much weight is given to the patterns revealed. Because EDA is performed by constructing many descriptions of the same data set, there is always the hazard that one or two will reveal patterns which owe more to chance than any genuine regularity in the phenomenon. If you look at a galaxy of data points from a sufficiently large number of positions, you may eventually find one view that reveals an interesting constellation. The multiplicity of attempts to impose a pattern on the data can lead, if you are sufficiently persistent, to the discovery of chance alignments. You will not be able to discriminate easily between those which are caused by the underlying dynamics of the phenomenon you are studying and those due simply to the haphazard arrangement of influences effected by variables extrinsic to the phenomenon.

For example, suppose you run a study on response times. You simply record, let us say, how long it takes subjects to press a key when a red square appears on a computer monitor. You invite participants to sign up for the study on whichever day of the week they wish. You run the study and compare male and female responses. There is no significant difference. You decide to explore the data. Among other things, you find that for participants who signed up on Monday, there was a significant difference between males and females. What do you conclude? It would be possible to construct a gleaming and complex theoretical edifice upon this observation. Perhaps, for instance, males and females are affected differently by having to return to work on a Monday, and this influences their performance on the task. Or perhaps there is something about the kind of person who signs up to participate in an experiment on a Monday? Or perhaps it rained on that Monday, and males and females respond differently to wet weather. Or perhaps it was mere chance. It just so happened that, say, the male subjects who turned up that day were on average slower than the females. The difference was just a chance feature of a particular sample.

There is no way to settle this question definitively using the data you have already gathered. For sure, further exploratory analysis can help to narrow down the alternatives. For example, you might have happened to record data about the weather on each day of the study. If it also rained on Wednesday, then the weather hypothesis will be less promising. In the end, however, you will need to design and run a further study if you want to evaluate any of your hypothetical explanations. For example, you might design an experiment in which day of the week is a variable and in which some measure of personality you believe is relevant gets recorded for each participant. If the result you found before is a symptom of a key mechanism, then it should reappear in the fresh sample.

The problem of multiplicity is a problem you may have encountered before in a different context. When a large number of significance tests is carried out on a data set, there is a risk that some will cross the threshold of statistical significance but which do not reflect reliable effects. For example, imagine that you assess a group of subjects on 15 different tests designed to measure personality or intelligence. You construct a correlation matrix to examine the relationships among these measures. For example, you might be interested to know whether introversion correlates positively with IQ. With 15 variables each correlated with 14 others, there will be 105 different correlations. The .05 significance level means that the statistic found is likely to occur by chance only five times in 100. However, now you have done about 100 correlations! You should expect five of them to reach the .05 significance level even if there are no reliable relationships among the variables. If, say, nine correlations do reach this criterion, you will have no way of discriminating between those which are reliable and those that are not. There are two possible solutions. One is to set a more severe criterion. This approach is discussed in detail in Chapter 8. The other is to attempt to replicate the finding in a fresh study. If there is a real relationship between intelligence and introversion, then it should appear again in the replication. Indeed, you would probably seek evidence that it was independent not only of the particular data sample, but also that it was independent of the particular instruments that you used. Thus, you would run further studies using different measures of intelligence and introversion. This approach will be developed further in Chapter 11 when we discuss reliability. Ultimately, replication is the best evidence that a result is reliable.

2.4 PRECISION Describe

Different ways of describing a given data set reveal different features of that data. An important thing to be able to do is to describe with precision patterns that are revealed. For example, to know that the number of years of education is positively related to salary in a particular country would be interesting. But to know by how much salary can be expected to increase (on average) for each additional year of study has even greater practical utility. A bank manager could use it in calculations of the credit worthiness of a student seeking a loan. The student could use it to assess the benefit of another year's study. And so on. Discovering the existence and direction of a relationship is interesting, but in a practical world it is important to go beyond that to find a more precise numerical description of the relationship which identifies the magnitude of the relationship as well.

An interesting example of this from psychology is Hick's law. Hick (1952) was interested in the time it takes subjects to respond when on each trial they must select one response from among several. His apparatus consisted of an array of lights, each with a corresponding button. At the start of each trial, all the lights were off. One light would come on. As quickly as possible, the subject had to press the corresponding button. The data are displayed in Fig. 2.3 The data show a positive relationship between the number of choices and the time taken to respond. The more possible choices, the longer subjects take to respond.

However, Hick was able to go further than this and provide a more precise description of the relationship. He transformed the data by taking the logarithm of each response time. When the log of response time is plotted against the number of choices available, the relationship shown in Fig. 2.4 becomes apparent. That is, as the number of choices increases, there is a linear increase in the log of the reaction time. This

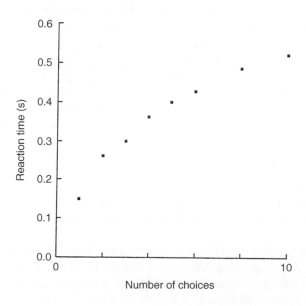

Figure 2.3   Choice reaction time raw data, adapted from Hicks (1952)

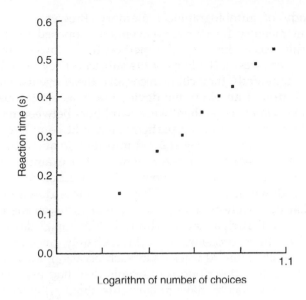

Figure 2.4 Log transformed choice reaction time data

straight line relationship makes the precise numerical relationship between the two variables clear. By transforming the raw data using logarithms, a more precise description has been obtained. We will see other situations where a transformation of data can be useful in Chapter 3.

2.5 SMOOTHING

Earlier in the chapter, we noted that a good description reveals relevant detail. The other side of this coin is that a good description omits irrelevant detail. In the following section, we examine a technique that emphasizes the extraction of patterns by removing irrelevant detail. Smoothing is especially useful when your data is a series of measurements made one after the other. For example, you might have recorded the fundamental frequency of an utterance once every 10 ms in order to view the way that intonation changes as a sentence is spoken (e.g. Hirst, 1983). You will probably be less interested in momentary fluctuations than general features such as whether the pitch rises or falls as the sentence finishes. Smoothing emphasizes these major patterns by eliminating detail.

The example that follows illustrates the application of smoothing to variations in the quality of memory for items that are related to the order the items were originally presented in. Brewer (1988) presents results from a study of autobiographical memory. Brewer was particularly interested in memory for everyday events as opposed to special occasions. For this reason, he devised a method that allowed him to record mundane occurrences in the lives of his subjects. They were later tested to see how confidently they could recognize these events. Each participant carried around an electronic device that was set to buzz them at random times. On average, there were two hours between these buzzes. When the buzzer went off, the participant would complete a response card. Among other things, they entered information about their physical actions at the time when the buzzer went off. For example, if you were a participant in such a study and your buzzer went off now, you would write 'sitting down and reading'. They also wrote down other details such as what they were thinking, but we will focus on the category of physical actions. Participants carried on like this for 17 days. Then they were tested on three occasions, once immediately, once after about 10 weeks and, finally, after 20 weeks. On each occasion, they were shown cards on which their descriptions of events they had experienced were written. Their task was to make judgements about whether they recognized the event. They rated the item from 1 to 7, with 1 meaning they could not remember it at all and 7 meaning they were certain that they remembered the event.

Figure 2.5 displays a copy of the plot of serial position effects that Brewer presented in his article. The plot here is slightly different because I read off the data values from the original by eye, and I have changed one of the axes. It shows the mean recognition rating for events plotted against the day of the study on which the subject originally experienced the event. Brewer draws attention to a pattern in this graph. There is, first, a primacy effect. That is, events occuring near the beginning of the study tend to be remembered better. Second, day six of the study was the day of an important celebration in the native culture, Thanksgiving. Events recorded that weekend seem to be better remembered.

The plot in Fig. 2.5 is a fairly good representation of Brewer's data. I do not mean to criticize it. However, it will provide a useful illustration for the application of a technique for making a pattern in data stand out more clearly. The actual data values used in our plots are given in Table 2.2.

The plot in Fig. 2.5 is a little jagged. These small perturbations can be removed by applying a smoothing procedure along the line. The procedure we will illustrate simply involves replacing each data value with the median of itself and its two neighbours. For example, the data point on day seven is 4.8. Its neighbours are 4.9 and 5.4, and so the replacement is the median of these, 4.9. The third column of the table shows the values obtained by applying this procedure right along the line. Note that the end points are simply copied forward. The final column applies the same procedure to column three in turn. Figure 2.6 plots the smoothed data in the final column. This plot abstracts a simplified

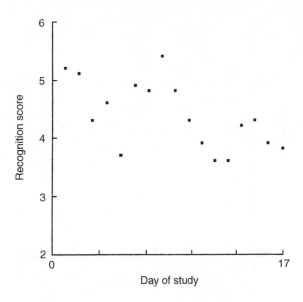

Figure 2.5 Time series plot of memory data, adapted from Brewer (1988)

Table 2.2 Brewer data, estimated from a graph in Brewer (1988), 'Memory for randomly sample autobiographical events', in U. Neisser & E. Winograd (Eds.) *Remembering reconsidered: Ecological and traditional approaches to the study of memory.* Cambridge, Cambridge University Press.

Day of study	Mean recognition	M[3] smooth	M[3] smooth twice
1	5.2	5.2	5.2
2	5.1	5.1	5.1
3	4.3	4.6	4.6
4	4.6	4.3	4.6
5	3.7	4.6	4.6
6	4.9	4.8	4.8
7	4.8	4.9	4.8
8	5.4	4.8	4.8
9	4.8	4.8	4.8
10	4.3	4.3	4.3
11	3.9	3.9	3.9
12	3.6	3.6	3.6
13	3.6	3.6	3.6
14	4.2	4.2	4.2
15	4.3	4.2	4.2
16	3.9	3.9	3.9
17	3.8	3.8	3.8

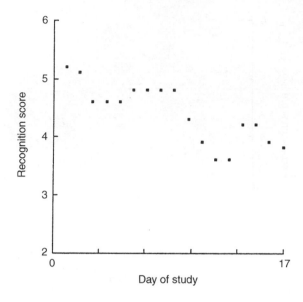

Figure 2.6　Smoothed time series plot of memory data

description of the data and, at least arguably, highlights key features more clearly.

2.6　WORKING GRAPHS VERSUS PUBLICATION GRAPHS

It is important to make a distinction between working graphs and publication graphs. Working graphs are created for yourself as you explore the data. There will be many of these. Their purpose is to help you discover regularities in the data. Publication graphs, on the other hand, appear in your final report. Their purpose is to help you convey your findings to the reader. There will be relatively few publication graphs. It is surprisingly uncommon for papers to contain more than a couple of graphs per experiment. Select graphs for your report carefully. Publication graphs should be deployed, like sentences, when they convey a point that you require for your argument.

2.7　TWO SIMPLE DESCRIPTIVE METHODS

Two techniques devised by Tukey have worked their way into the standard repertoire of descriptive statistics. You are probably familiar

```
 6      1 3
 7      3
 8   H  5 8
 9   M  1 3 5
10   H  3 5 6 7
11      9
```

Figure 2.7   Stem and leaf plot of acallosal IQ scores

with box and whisker plots and stem and leaf diagrams already. But since they will be mentioned frequently in later chapters, I will briefly review them here.

Stem and leaf diagrams represent data using a mixture of numbers and graphical techniques. I list below a small data set that we will use for illustration. The values are the verbal IQ s of 13 subjects with agenesis of the corpus callosum. This condition arises as a congenital malformation of the brain. It was once thought that the intellectual performance of such subjects was inevitably impaired. However, modern scanning techniques have been able to identify cases that have good levels of cognitive function. Such cases were not likely to be identified previously because they did not present for neuropsychological testing. The data here is taken from Sauerwein, Nolin and Lassonde (1994).

Verbal IQ: 107,63,61,93,85,105,119,106,73,91,95,103,88

Figure 2.7 displays the data as a stem and leaf diagram. The diagram is constructed by splitting each data point into two numbers: the stem and the leaf. The column of numbers at the left of the diagram is the stem. The leaves are laid out in order to the right of the corresponding stem. For example, the stem of 73 is 7; its leaf is 3. The row below represents two data points: 85 and 88. They are on the same row because they have the same stem. The stem and leaf diagram has the shape of a histogram that has been turned round. Like a histogram, it conveys the distribution of scores across the range of values. However, it also contains information about the specific numerical values that are present in the sample. A histogram shows only the frequency of cases in each bin. The stem and leaf diagram preserves the original data completely. Figure 2.7 contains some other information. Particular rows are annotated with letters. These letters indicate the presence of key data points on the given row. For example, M indicates that the median lies on that row. The letter II indicates that one of the hinges lies on the row. The hinges are the quartiles of the sample. Each is the data point mid-way in the rank ordering between the median and either the maximum or the minimum data point in the sample.

Figure 2.8 displays the same data using a box and whisker plot. The limits of the box are the hinges of the sample. The line through the

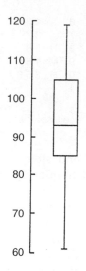

Figure 2.8   Box and whisker plot of acallosal IQ scores

middle of the box marks the median. The whiskers in this case have been drawn to the maximum and minimum values in the sample. The box and whisker plot provides a convenient way to describe the distribution of data in a sample.

2.8   SUMMARY

Data analysis is there to help you understand the phenomenon you want to study. It is a process in which you combine exploration of the data to search for patterns with tests of specific hypotheses. The distinction between exploratory and confirmatory techniques is not always clear cut. When confirmatory techniques are used to build models, they can be viewed as creating a description of the data. Exploratory techniques raise questions and sometimes it is necessary to carry out a new study to evaluate those questions. A description or model of a data set is better when it is simple, quantitatively precise and when it reveals relevant regularities.

3 DATA SCREENING

An important phase of the data analysis process is data screening. Screening involves examination of the raw data and residuals for patterns or features that can influence either the choice of statistical tests or the legitimacy of inferences based on the data analysis. Statistical methods generally make some assumptions about data to which they are applied. If a data set does not meet the assumptions then it can be inappropriate to use the test. In particular, inferential statistics can be misleading if used on data that do not satisfy the assumptions of a test.

The assumptions made in general are concerned with the distribution of data in the population that the sample is drawn from. Each data set is expected to be similar to the prototype of the normal distribution. The artithmetic used in many tests assumes that the distribution of data in the population is like the normal distribution. These tests rely on this assumption especially when they compare one sample with another. The statistical comparison between the samples focuses on one feature of the samples, typically the sample mean, and assumes that all the other features of the samples are held constant. As long as the distributional properties of the samples are similar and, ideally, as long as they are all close to the normal distribution, the comparison made by the test is valid. If there are discrepancies, however, the comparison may not make much sense.

There are five things that should be checked which we will examine in this chapter. They are whether the distributions are skewed, whether they have unequal variance, whether the distribution of residuals represents random error, whether there are outliers and whether there is missing data.

3.1 SKEW

Consider the three samples displayed in Table 3.1. The distribution of data in each sample is shown in Fig. 3.1. The median of S3 and N3 is 3, the median of N5 is 5. However, *t*-tests suggest that the means of S3 and

Table 3.1　Artificial data

N5	N3	S3
3	1	1
3	1	2
4	2	2
4	2	2
4	2	3
4	2	3
5	3	3
5	3	3
5	3	3
5	3	3
5	3	4
5	3	4
6	4	4
6	4	5
6	4	11
7	4	4
7	5	12
7	5	7

N3 are significantly different, t (17) = 2.374, $p < .05$, but that S3 and N5 are not significantly different, t (17) = 1.59, $p > .01$). Because S3 is so badly skewed the t-test is misleading.

Figure 3.2 shows why skewed samples can create difficulties for comparisons. Figure 3.2(a) shows two samples which are normally distributed. The means lie at the peak of the distribution, and it will be

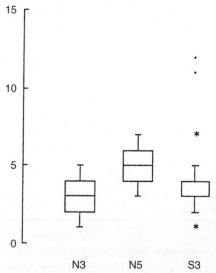

Figure 3.1　Comparison of the distribution of data in three artificial samples

easy for a test like the *t*-test to differentiate them. However, Fig. 3.2(b) shows two further samples whose distributions are skewed in opposite directions. The sample with lower scores (on the left) is positively skewed. The other sample is negatively skewed. The extreme scores in these long tails have the effect of dragging the means of each sample

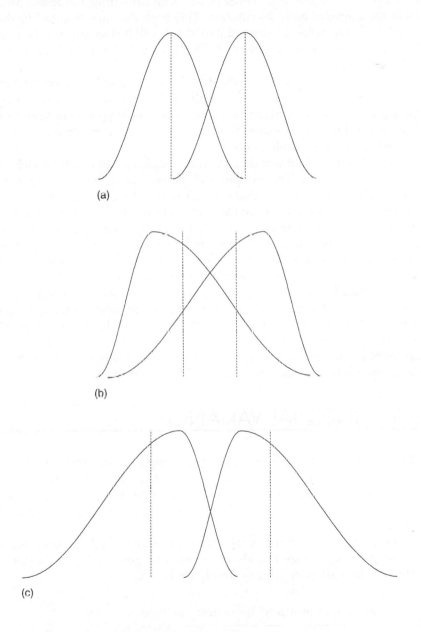

(a)

(b)

(c)

Figure 3.2   The effect of skewed distributions on contrasts between means

away from the peak of the distribution. In this example, the means are drawn towards one another. Because the means are now closer together, they will be more difficult for the *t*-test to differentiate.

Similarly, Fig. 3.2(c) compares two samples which are skewed so that they appear 'back to back'. Again, they are skewed in opposite directions. Again, the extreme scores in the long tails drag the mean away from the centre of each distribution. This time they are dragged further apart. If two samples are skewed like this, it will be too easy for the *t*-test to declare their means are different. There is a risk that a significant *t*-test will be misleading.

You cannot usually examine the distribution of data in the population, because you have access to data only in the sample you have taken. However, you can look at the distribution of data in your sample and use that as a guide. To the extent that you have a representative sample, it can serve as a reasonable guide.

You will always find that data in your sample do not exactly match the normal distribution. The sample will depart from this ideal to some extent. Statisticians believe that tests such as the *t*-test and ANOVA can tolerate small departures from this assumption. That is, the *p*-value they produce will still be accurate even if the groups they compare are not exactly normally distributed. These statistics are said to be robust with respect to this assumption. When you screen your data to check this assumption, you have to judge whether the extent to which the assumption is violated is small enough to tolerate. This is a subjective judgement that requires experience and confidence. However, when you check your data, look especially to make sure that none of the groups you are comparing are skewed in opposite directions. If they are skewed in opposite directions, as we saw earlier, there is a large risk that the *p*-value produced by a statistical test will be incorrect.

3.2   UNEQUAL VARIANCE

The assumption that the groups being compared are distributed similarly also requires that the variance of each group is broadly similar. Their variances will never be exactly the same, but if they differ too greatly, the inferences suggested by statistics like the *t*-test or ANOVA may be incorrect.

It is possible to use a statistical test to determine whether the variances of two groups are significantly different. You can use Bartlett's test to compare the variances. This is simply an *F*-ratio:

$$F_{max} = \frac{\text{variance of group with greatest variance}}{\text{variance of group with least variance}}$$

If the two variances are equal, then F_{max} will be 1. The bigger the difference, the larger F_{max} will be. If F_{max} is significant, the difference between the variances is unlikely to be attributable entirely to chance. Whether it is significant can be determined by checking in tables for the F statistic. The numerator degrees of freedom is 1, the denominator degrees of freedom is $n - 1$, where n is the number of cases in each group. If F_{max} is significant, then you can say with confidence that the variances of the groups are not equal.

Statistics like the *t*-test and ANOVA, as noted earlier, are thought to be robust with respect to this assumption. That means that mild departures from the assumption will not lead to incorrect results. Even if F_{max} is significant, the data may be alright. As a rule of thumb, if F_{max} is not greater than 4 then the departure from the assumption is acceptable. However, if the number of cases in the samples being compared is unequal, then F_{max} should not exceed 2.

3.3 RANDOM ERROR

When you use a statistical test, you are applying a statistical model to the data. You assume that the explanatory variables you include in the model account for all the systematic variation in the data. This assumption can be tested by examining the distribution of residuals. The difference between the value predicted by the model for each case and the observed value is the residual. Statistics like the *t*-test and ANOVA assume that what the model cannot account for is random error: just noise in the data. If this assumption is correct, then the residuals should be distributed randomly. To be precise, the distribution of residuals should be a random normal distribution with a mean of zero. This assumption is known as the normality assumption.

Many statistics programs will save residuals when you fit a model. By displaying the residuals, you can check this assumption. If your choice of model is correct, then your explanatory variables will account for all the systematic variation in the data. When you look at the residuals, there should be no systematic variation left.

As well as allowing you to test the assumptions of your test, examining residuals can play a valuable role as a component of exploratory data analysis. An analogy can be drawn once more here with an example from the physical sciences. Recall the discussion of data, error and residuals in Chapter 1. The residual is the bit left over after you have accounted for the data using your existing model. The factors you use account for some proportion of the variance; the residual is the remaining variance. Marie Curie, the Polish scientist, discovered radium by observing that after she had accounted for all the constituents of a piece of coal that were already known, there was some residual mass. She embarked on a series of studies in which she physically decomposed a sample of coal until she isolated the residue. Often, important scientific discoveries depend on initially noting a discrepancy between predictions made by the existing model and the observed data. In Curie's work, existing theory accounted for her initial observations in part, but some of the mass was unaccounted for. Her research was important because she followed through her observation with experiments that led to the discovery of a new element.

In psychology, very often the model that is fitted to the data will not exhaust the systematic variation. Things affect the outcome that were not included in the model. Human behaviour is rich and is influenced by variables that are not always anticipated when a study is planned. The effect of any variable that influenced scores but was not included in your model may remain in the residuals. The residuals contain all variation not accounted for by the model. It is possible to pull out systematic variation contained in the residuals. Simply by checking whether the residual score correlates with variables not included in the model, you can test whether those variables had a systematic influence. If they did, then there will be a correlation between their values and the residuals.

When these distributional assumptions are not satisfied, the result of inferential tests may be of dubious value. A number of techniques are available for checking whether a sample does satisfy the assumptions of a given test, and there are a few methods for repairing samples that violate assumptions. The main tools in checking assumptions are graphical techniques. There are few good general purpose significance tests that are really helpful in checking assumptions. Samples that do not meet assumptions can be dealt with by transforming all the scores in a way that brings them into line, or by using non-parametric tests instead.

3.4   OUTLIERS

Outliers are data values that are extreme compared to other values obtained in a sample. Because of the arithmetic used in statistics like the *t*-test or ANOVA, outliers can have a disproportionate influence on the result. It is therefore important to discover whether there are outliers in your data and to decide how to deal with them.

There are a number of ways that extreme pieces of data can appear in your sample, and the way you deal with them depends to some extent on why you think they have occurred. There are four main ways they can occur that we will consider.

First, they can occur by chance. Although extreme values are rare, they do occur in the population, and it is possible that your sample just happens to have included an extreme case. If this is correct, then there is no principled reason to omit this case from the analysis.

Second, outliers can occur because of clerical errors of one kind or another. It is very easy to make a few mistakes when you transcribe scores from a paper record and enter them in a computer file. Sometimes these errors will show up as outliers. When you find an outlier, it is worth checking that the correct data value was recorded. Occasionally, it may be clear that the value is wrong because it is outside the range of scores possible on your variable. For example, if you administered a questionnaire or test whose maximum score is 30, but a score of, say, 56, has been recorded for one case, then you can be confident there has been an error in recording the score.

Where you can identify a clerical error, then the appropriate course of action is to enter the correct score, if you can. If you are unable to do this because the original score has been lost, then delete the outlier and treat it as missing data. Ways of dealing with missing data are described in Section 3.5.

Computer programs which administer experiments often automatically make checks on the data they record. For example, in response time experiments, where the speed of a subject's response is recorded, software may not record responses below some threshold (say, 50 ms). These trials are recorded as missing data. This is done where such quick responses are not plausible and where such a short time almost certainly represents an error or anticipation by the subject. The obvious hazard is that genuine data is excluded. Indeed, something like this happened when the NASA satellite monitoring ozone over Antarctica refused to pass on observations indicating that the ozone was being depleted. The extremely low readings were outside the range that the software had been programmed to accept as plausible.

A third way in which an outlier can appear in your sample is if you accidentally sample a case from a different population than the one you are interested in. For example, imagine you are interested in memory and you sign up 20 volunteers to do an experiment. You may accidentally sign up a subject who is not a member of the adult population of normal people whose memory you want to understand. You might accidentally recruit someone with Korsakoff's syndrome. This is a condition that afflicts some chronic alcoholics. Because of a vitamin deficiency linked to alcoholism, their hypothalamus does not function normally, and this affects memory. If you are able to establish that a particular case in the sample is not a member of the population you intend to study, then you should exclude their data.

Finally, you can have outliers in your data because the population you are studying turns out not to be normally distributed. If the population data is positively skewed, for example, then very high scores will be more common. This is because a larger proportion of the population lies out in the positive tail, and there is more chance that a random sample will contain such cases. You need good evidence to make a convincing argument that the source of your outlier is an underlying population that is not normally distributed. You could make this argument if previous research across a number of different samples consistently reveals a distinct distribution, or if you can marshall a theoretical argument that explains why you would not expect the population distribution to be normal.

Reaction times are positively skewed in many experimental settings. In some fields of cognitive psychology, such as psycholinguistics, reaction time data is often log transformed before analysis to make the distribution of data conform better to the assumptions of ANOVA. The log transformation has the effect of pulling in the long tail.

3.5   MISSING VALUES

Sometimes data goes missing. For example, a subject may fail to complete some items in a questionnaire, equipment may break down at a crucial moment or errors may be made in recording the data. There are several ways to deal with this. Here are the most straightforward alternatives.

3.5.1 Do not try to replace the data

In a regression or correlation study this means deleting all the data for a given subject if any of her data are missing. For example, if you are doing a multiple regression study of spelling ability, and you have gathered data on, say, 10 variables for each subject, but you find that Sally's 'reading age' score is missing, then you would delete Sally from the sample. (This is called listwise deletion.) This is obviously a touch extravagant, since it probably took a lot of time to gather the data and so forth.

In an ANOVA problem, missing data which is not replaced 'unbalances the design'. This means that there are now different numbers of subjects in each condition. The consequence is that the *F*-tests are less robust. They become more sensitive to violations of the assumptions of homogeneity of variance and so on. For example, you cannot afford to tolerate such large differences in within cell variances if the design is unbalanced. If the amount of missing data is small, and so long as it is not going missing systematically, deletion is reasonable.

3.5.2 Delete the variable

This is viable in a multiple regression situation. If you find that, say, several reading age scores are missing, then you could consider omitting reading age from the analysis. Just leave it out of the model. You would only do this if either:

- you thought reading age was anyway not very important and you could live without it; or
- you thought the reading age measure was a bit redundant because it correlated highly with other variables for which you did have complete data.

3.5.3 Replace the missing data with the mean

You can use the mean of the rest of the sample to estimate Sally's missing reading age score. This assumes that Sally is a typical pupil, and so the most likely score for her to get is the class mean. Using the mean is a cautious move, because the mean of the sample is not changed. In ANOVA situations, an alternative is to replace a missing value with the appropriate within cell mean. For example, if you had a 2×2 design, there would be four cells each with its own mean. Missing data in each cell is replaced by the mean for that cell. Using the cell mean rather than the grand mean is a good approach.

3.5.4 Take a bath

When you land in hot water, take a bath. Use the observation that some data is missing as data in itself. Perhaps the fact that subjects have refused to answer a particular item, or teachers have refused to report a particular score for some pupils, is valuable information in itself. Invent a new variable called, for example, 'omitted', and give each subject a score on this new variable. The score might be the number of items the subject omitted altogether. This new variable can then be added to the model.

3.6 TRANSFORMING DATA

Several times above, we have discussed transforming data. The general idea is to change the value of each score in the sample in a similar way.

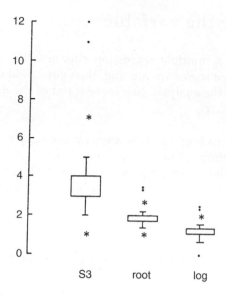

Figure 3.3　Comparison of the distribution of data in S3 following transformation

If we choose a good change, the new sample will look more like a normal distribution. Transformations can be useful if the assumptions of a test are seriously violated. As an example, recall the distribution S3. We can transform this by taking the square root or the log of each value. Box and whisker plots displaying the transformed data are shown in Fig. 3.3. The transformations improve the symmetry of the distribution. If you do a *t*-test comparing log transformed data for N5 and S3, i.e. you transform both, the difference is significant, t (17) $\times$ 3.44, $p < .01$.

Transforming data can also overcome problems in the distribution of residuals or violations of homogeneity of within cell variances. The process of trying a particular transformation is very much one of trial and error. Try transforming the data using your chosen transformation, but always remember to check and see that the transformation has actually worked. If it has not worked, if the problems are still there, then you can try a different transformation. Tabachnik and Fidell (1989, p. 85) provide a useful guide to the selection of appropriate transformations.

3.7　DATA SCREENING FOR ANOVA

In practical terms, there are two phases to data screening in ANOVA. The first step involves examining the values of the dependent variable. Plots are made of the distribution of the raw scores gathered from subjects, and these graphs are examined. Then, once the model has been fitted to the data, the residuals are checked. This second stage is sometimes called model adequacy checking. If the statistical model is inadequate — if, perhaps, an important variable was omitted — then the effect of the omitted factor can sometimes be seen in the residuals.

3.7.1 Raw scores

An important assumption of ANOVA is that the distribution of scores in each cell of the design is broadly similar. This is usually checked by looking at the variance of scores within each cell. A first step is to construct box plots for each cell. The experimenter likes to see the box plots line up broadly in parallel. The box plots should indicate a similar spread of values in each cell. Box plots can also show up extreme values in a cell. These values are called outliers, and we have to take care over these because outliers can have a large influence on the outcome of tests. Finally, box plots can also be used to check that scores in each cell are symmetrically distributed. Figure 3.1 indicates that for N3 the scores are symmetrically distributed, but in S3 they are positively skewed.

The cell variances can be compared directly. In general, as a rule of thumb, if the number of cases in each cell is the same for all cells, the F-tests are safe as long as the largest within cell variance is no more than four times bigger than the smallest. If there are unequal numbers of cases in each cell, the F-tests are not so robust. Nevertheless, if the largest cell variance is no more than double the smallest the results are typically reliable.

The distribution of scores in each cell can be displayed using histograms. However, while histograms are good for checking the symmetry of distributions, they are more helpful when the sample size is fairly large.

At an early stage it is useful simply to plot the cell means. This gives you the first indication of the results of the experiment, and is very helpful when it comes to interpreting the ANOVA. In general, you should plot the mean of each cell against its variance. If all cells have broadly the same variance, there is no special pattern in this plot. However, it is common to find that variance is linearly related to the cell mean. That is, cells with bigger means tend to have larger variances. If (when!) you find this, you ought to consider transforming the data so that this relationship is removed. Appropriate transformations to consider in this situation are changing scores to their logs or to their square root. If you get a negative relationship between the mean and variance, consider squaring the raw scores.

3.7.2 Residuals

In a two-way ANOVA, the model M3.1 is used.

M3.1 data $= P1 + P2 + P1 * P2 +$ error

This model suggests that each score can be understood in terms of the two predictor variables and their interaction. However, the model's estimate for each piece of data will be slightly different from the observed value. This discrepancy between the estimate and the actual data is known as the residual. The residuals represent the error in the model. If the model is basically adequate, that is if the model contains the important factors that actually are influencing scores in the experimental situation, then the error should be entirely due to random effects. There should be no systematic patterns in the residuals. There should be just as many overestimates as underestimates, and therefore, on the average, the errors should cancel out and average zero. When you check the residuals, you check first that they are distributed in the expected way and second that they do not correlate with any variables not included in the model.

The distribution of residuals can be checked easily by doing a stem and leaf plot. This plot should be centered on zero, and it should be symmetrical about this centre. Ideally, the stem and leaf plot of residuals has the shape of a normal distribution. Well, we can dream. Another way to check the distribution of residuals is to use a normal probability plot. Such plots directly compare the distribution of residuals with a true normal distribution. If the assumption is met, the line of points follows the diagonal of the graph. Deviation from the diagonal indicates a departure from the assumption. Of course, normal probability plots can be used with raw scores as well as with residuals. Figures 3.4 and 3.5 are normal probability plots for N3 and S3 respectively, the samples given above. You can see how the skewed data set produces a different pattern in Figure 3.5.

Residuals should be plotted against estimates. Estimates are the values the model predicts for each data point. In ANOVA these correspond to cell means. Plotting residuals against estimates will let you check that the residuals fall fairly evenly above and below zero. Second, however, you can check that the spread of the residuals about zero is fairly even for all sizes of estimate. What you can find is that the variance of residuals is related linearly to estimates, so that as the estimate rises, the spread of the residuals increases. In other words, when estimated scores are larger, the accuracy of the estimate is poorer. This pattern is shown in Fig. 3.6.

The problem here is similar to the problem of linear relationships between cell means and variances, and can be dealt with in the same way (see Section 3.7.1). By transforming the raw data and re-running the

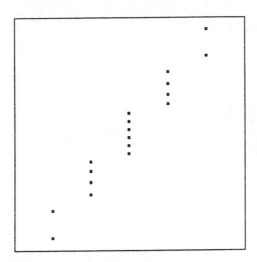

Figure 3.4 Normal probability plot of a sample that is roughly normally distributed

ANOVA using the transformed scores instead of the original raw data, you can overcome the difficulty. If your plot of residuals against estimates looks like Fig 3.6, try taking the log or the square root of each score.

Residuals can also be plotted against other variables. For example, it can be interesting to plot the residuals against the day subjects were tested. In many experiments, subjects are tested over several days and we assume that the day of the week is not systematically influencing

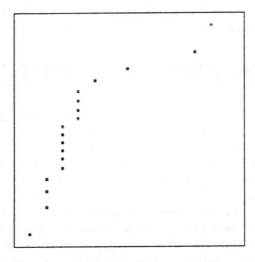

Figure 3.5 Normal probability plot of a sample that is skewed

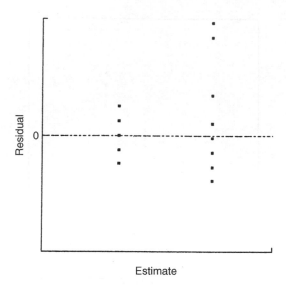

Figure 3.6   Plot of estimates against residuals

results. One way to check this assumption would be to plot residuals for each score against the day of the week the score was obtained. If the assumption is correct, then the distribution of residuals should be the same for each day of the week. However, if we find for instance that residuals are all positive on Monday (i.e. the model systematically underestimates scores on Monday) then we have a clue that day of the week may be having an influence on scores. If there genuinely is a systematic effect of this kind, then we need either to get this variable into the model or else to control it properly by, for example, testing all subjects on the same day.

3.8   DATA SCREENING IN A REPORT

The process of data screening is time consuming and generates a large quantity of graphs, tables and figures. While data screening is necessary, it is unglamorous and will merit only a passing mention in the write-up of a project. You should state clearly and concisely which checks have been made, and which have proved satisfactory. It is especially important to record in the results section any transformations of the data, any outliers, together with information about how you dealt with them, and how much missing data there was, and how it was handled. When reporting the results of any inferential statistic, be sure there is no ambiguity about whether it was performed on transformed or untransformed data. If you tried a transformation but decided to go ahead and use the raw data after all, it is probably worth briefly mentioning why you decided not to transform the data. Draw a clear distinction between working graphs and publication graphs. In analysing the results, you will produce several graphs at different stages of the analysis. In the results section of a project report you would present only the most important, the most telling of the graphs.

Usually the best way to deal with uncertainty (are the assumptions met, or not?; should I transform the data, or not?) is the least elegant: do the analysis twice, once one way and then again another way. For example, you might analyse the raw data and then analyse transformed data. Once both analyses are done, you can compare the inferences. If both approaches agree in terms of the inferences they would lead you to draw, then you need not worry. If they disagree, you are probably safer with the transformed scores.

3.9 SUMMARY

An inferential statistic is a piece of reasoning. It runs: if certain assumptions are made about the populations being compared, then effects of the observed size have such and such a probability of arising if the null hypothesis is correct. However, this argument depends on the assumptions made being at least approximately correct. These assumptions can be evaluated for practical purposes by examining the sample data. Tests like ANOVA appear to be tolerant of mild violations of the assumptions, but if more than one assumption is violated this may not hold. Sometimes violations of assumptions can be ameliorated by subjecting data to a transformation, but the investigator needs to consider the effect of transformation on the interpretation of findings.

4 ANALYSIS OF VARIANCE

You will undoubtedly have encountered ANOVA before. This chapter begins by reviewing the fundamentals of this statistical technique. Later we will look at analyses involving more than one variable. However, we start with a one-way analysis which examines the effect of varying the levels of a single factor, or predictor variable.

Developmental psychologists are interested in which words children learn to use first. One frequent observation is that a particular kind of word, the basic level word, seems to be used most often by younger children. Basic level words are words like 'dog' or 'car'. Basic level words are less general than superordinate level nouns, such as 'vehicle' or 'animal', but not as specific as subordinate level nouns such as 'mini' or 'dalmation'. Waxman and Hatch (1992) investigated whether pre-school children could be induced to use superordinate or subordinate labels to describe objects. They hypothesized that, in fact, they would use such terms if the context was appropriate. In their study, they showed children photographs of everyday objects, such as a dog. They then asked questions like 'Is this a cat?' or 'Is this a flower?'. They predicted that children might reply using a label at the same level as the noun in the question. For example, if they were asked whether the dog was a flower, they might reply 'No, it is an animal' if they could use superordinate level nouns.

The data in Table 4.1 is artificial. However, it is broadly comparable to that reported in Waxman and Hatch (1992). The original study investigated only the two younger age groups. I have fictitiously added a third for illustration only. Each child was given three questions for each of eight photographs. The three questions aimed to elicit a subordinate level noun, a basic level noun, and a superordinate level noun respectively. A child scored if they produced a noun at the appropriate level. They could thus score a maximum of three for each photograph. The scores in Table 4.1 are the mean number of nouns produced for each photograph. There are nine imaginary children in each age group.

One question of interest is whether older children tend to produce a greater variety of nouns under these conditions. If they do, then the mean number of nouns produced will be greater for the older age groups. Table 4.2 suggests that this is so. However, it is necessary to

Table 4.1 Mean number of labels produced by each child

Age 3	Age 4	Age 5
1.625	2.250	2.250
2.250	1.875	1.875
1.625	2.250	2.500
1.750	1.625	2.125
1.875	2.375	2.500
1.500	2.125	2.375
1.375	2.000	2.625
1.625	2.500	2.475
1.500	1.625	1.875

levels

establish whether the difference between the groups is merely the result
of chance differences in performance. This, you will be aware, is where
ANOVA comes in.

The performance of individual children varies: they do not all get the
same score. In particular, we are considering whether the age of a child
affects their score. However, there are many things other than age which
can influence these differences. For example, whether a particular child
was up late watching cartoons last night, or whether they were distracted during testing. These chance differences, termed error variance,
are inevitable. ANOVA tests whether the effect of an explanatory variable, such as age, is distinguishable from error variance.

Variance within each age group will be just error variance. If age does
not influence performance, then you also expect that the only differences
between children in different age groups will be chance differences. That
is, the between-group variance will be no different to within group
variance. ANOVA compares the variation between different age groups
to variation within the same age group. If the between-groups variance is
greater than the within groups variance, then the effect of the variable is
greater than the effect of error variance.

Table 4.3 shows the analysis of variance for this data. The variance,
usually termed mean square, for the effect of age is 0.854. The variance
for error is 0.081. Obviously, the effect of age is greater than error
variance.

Table 4.2 Number of labels produced
by different age groups

Age	Mean	SD
3	1.68	0.26
4	2.07	0.31
5	2.29	0.28

Table 4.3   Analysis of number of labels produced

Source	SS	df	MS	F	p
Age	1.708	2	0.854	10.597	0.001
Error	1.935	24	0.081		

These differences could have arisen as a result merely of chance sampling differences. For example, it could happen by chance that more of the children in one age group were up late the previous evening. The probability of getting data like this if the differences between age groups really were just chance sampling differences can be calculated exactly. An F-ratio is calculated by dividing the mean square for age by the mean square for error:

$$F = 0.854/0.081$$
$$= 10.597$$

The value calculated for F is then compared against the critical value for F in tables. You have to take into account both the degrees of freedom associated with the numerator of the F-ratio (in this case, 2) and the degrees of freedom associated with the denominator (in this case, 24) when you look up the tables. You will find relevant tables at the back of most introductory statistics textbooks.

The model that this ANOVA tests can be described with an equation.

M4.1: score = constant + age + error

This equation says that children's scores can be understood as being made up of three parts. The first, the *constant*, is the mean score of all children participating. The overall mean for this sample of 27 fictitious children was 2.01. The second part is an effect that can be attributed to *age*: older children tend to get higher scores. The final part is *error* variance: each individual score has a residual component that can only be attributed to chance variation. These last two parts are worthy of detailed consideration.

The effect of the variable, *age*, is summarized using three numbers, one for each level of the variable. Technically, these numbers are termed parameters of the model. They are simply the difference between the overall mean and the mean of each group. For example, the mean for four year-olds is 2.07, and so the effect for that level of age is $(2.07 - 2.01) = +0.06$. In words, being four years old has the effect, on average, of raising your score by 0.06 above the overall mean. Effects for the other levels can be calculated in the same way.

three year-olds $= 1.68-2.01 = -0.33$
four year-olds $= 2.07-2.01 = +0.06$
five year-olds $= 2.29-2.01 = +0.28$

Thus, the score for the first three year-old listed in Table 4.1, which was 1.625, is modelled as:

score = constant + effect of being three + error

or

$1.625 = 2.01-0.33 +$ error

The remaining part of the score, the *error*, is often termed the residual. It is simply the difference between the actual score a child got and the mean score in their group. For this child, the value of the residual is -0.055. You are encouraged to satisfy yourself that this is correct.

4.1   ASSUMPTIONS OF ANOVA

Like most tests, ANOVA procedures make certain assumptions about the data. The significance tests that ANOVA provides are strictly accurate only if the data conforms to these assumptions. In practice, data never conforms exactly to the assumptions and, indeed, it is impossible to directly test all of the assumptions. Nevertheless, it is appropriate to examine the data to ensure that it conforms at least roughly.

In Chapter 3 we looked at data screening in some detail. Here, the process is briefly illustrated in relation to a specific example. First, there is no missing data. That is one advantage of generating it artificially. Next, side by side box and whisker plots, displayed in Fig. 4.1, show the distribution of data in the three groups.

The standard deviation of the three groups was broadly similar, as you saw in Table 4.2. The box and whisker plots confirm that the distribution of scores in each group is broadly the same. Furthermore, none of the three groups shows a markedly skewed distribution. Although we cannot test directly whether the distribution of scores in the population is normal or that the population variances are homogenous, the box and whisker plots provide reassurance that there is no gross departure from these assumptions.

A plot of variance against group mean does not indicate any untoward relationship (Fig. 4.2).

One child in the youngest age group appears as an outlier. Their score is relatively extreme compared to the rest of the group. However, there is no more reason to question the validity of this datum than any of the others, and so we will retain their score. If you wanted to be cautious, you could delete the score and confirm that the ANOVA still showed age to be a significant effect. You can try that as an exercise.

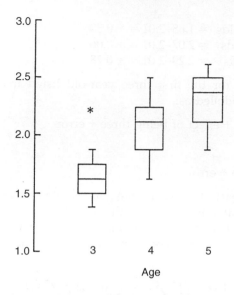

Figure 4.1   Distribution of labelling scores for three age groups

Finally, the residuals are plotted to examine their distribution (Fig. 4.3). The normal probability plot shows the residuals roughly normally distributed. There is no cause for concern. This process of model adequacy testing could proceed more exhaustively, as outlined in Chapter 3. However, the example will not be taken further at this point.

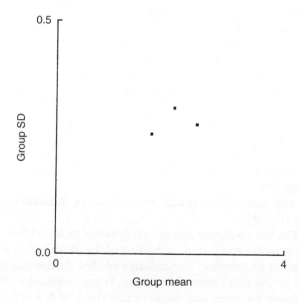

Figure 4.2   Relationship between mean and SD

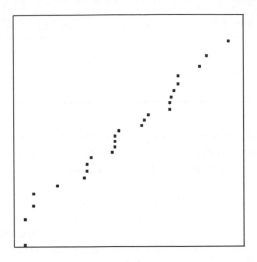

Figure 4.3 Normal probability plot for residuals

4.2 TWO-WAY ANOVA

In Waxman and Hatch's study of children's ability to use labels, we used only one predictor variable to account for scores. The only predictor was age. A design with just one independent variable can be described as a one-way design. Often, however, it is useful to employ more than one predictor. In this section, we will look at an example in which two variables are used.

Baddeley (1993) describes an unpublished study carried out with Robbins and others, in which the ability of chess players to recall the positions of pieces on a board mid-way through a game was compared. The following description is based loosely on the study they report. A board was set up with pieces arranged in positions taken from a real game. Each player was shown the board for 10 seconds. Then the board was hidden. The players' task was to set out pieces on an empty board exactly as they had been arranged on the board they had just seen. A player scored one point for each piece they placed correctly, and lost one for each piece they placed incorrectly. Two independent variables were employed. First, one group of subjects were relatively inexperienced players, while a second group were more expert. Second, half the subjects in each group had to perform a concurrent task. These subjects had to repeat the word 'the' aloud continuously while reconstructing the board.

This design has two predictors. First, there is chess playing skill. This predictor has two levels: inexperienced or expert. The second predictor is whether there is a concurrent task. This also has two levels: no concurrent task or a concurrent task of articulatory suppression (AS). Table

Table 4.4   Cells in two-way design for chess study

	Inexperienced	Expert
No concurrent task	1	2
Say 'the, the . . .'	3	4

4.4 shows the four different groups in the design. It is known from earlier studies that more skilful players do better on this task (de Groot, 1965). Therefore, we would expect that groups 2 and 4 will perform better than groups 1 and 3.

Continuously repeating the word 'the' is intended to occupy a component of working memory which Baddeley terms the articulatory loop. If this mechanism plays a role in setting out the remembered position, then scores will be poorer when this task is performed concurrently. That is, groups 1 and 2 will be expected to do worse than groups 3 and 4. Artificial data corresponding roughly to the results reported by Baddeley are listed in Table 4.5. Table 4.6 shows the mean for each group.

It is clear that groups 2 and 4, the experts, have done rather better than the experienced players. However, it also seems that there is very little difference between participants with no concurrent task and those subjected to articulatory suppression. ANOVA allows you to test whether these differences are statistically significant. Table 4.7 shows the ANOVA for this data.

The main effect of *skill* is significant. However, scores for the group given the concurrent task are not significantly worse. This suggests that the articulatory loop may not be important in the task of remembering chess positions. The ANOVA table also shows an interaction term. In this example, the interaction is not significant. The interaction tests whether

Table 4.5   Raw data for chess study

	Inexperienced	Expert
No concurrent task	1, 3, −2 2, 0, 1	10, 7, 11, 9, 12, 12
Say 'the, the . . .'	4, 2, −1, 1, 0, −1	9, 5, 7 11, 12, 14

Table 4.6   Cell means for chess study

	Inexperienced	Expert
No concurrent task	0.83	10.17
Say 'the, the . . .'	0.83	9.67

Table 4.7 Two-way analysis of chess study

Source	SS	df	MS	F	p
Skill (S)	495.042	1	495.042	91.816	0.001
Task (T)	0.375	1	0.375	0.070	0.795
S × T	0.375	1	0.375	0.070	0.795
Error	107.833	20	5.392		

the effect of each predictor is the same at each level of the other predictor. In this example, because there is no significant interaction, we can conclude that the effect of articulatory suppression is the same for both levels of skill.

The model for this two-way ANOVA can be described as:

M4.2 score = constant + skill + concurrent task
+ skill * concurrent task + error

The *skill * concurrent task* term is the interaction between the two predictors. The next section considers in some detail examples of two-way ANOVA in which the interaction term is significant.

4.3   INTERACTION

We use a data set based on experiments described by Schachter, Goldman and Gordon (1968). Schachter *et al.* were interested in the relationship between physiological hunger and appetite. Participants attended his laboratory, and when they arrived they were asked to wait in a small room. On the table was a plate of cookies. Although participants did not realize at the time, they were being observed. The dependent variable was the number of cookies they ate. Two predictor variables were used in the study. The first was whether participants were obese or not, and the second was whether they had eaten shortly before being offered the cookies. This is, therefore, a two-way design. The four cells are indicated in Table 4.8.

The design of this study suggests ANOVA is an appropriate test. Weight and hunger are variables we can use to explain differences between scores obtained by participants in the different groups. With

Table 4.8 Design of obesity study

	Normal weight	Obese
Recently fed	1	2
Obese	3	4

Table 4.9   Main effect of weight

	Normal weight	→	Obese
Recently fed	1		2
Starved	3		4

two factors, obviously, this is a two-way ANOVA problem. A two-way ANOVA tests three effects. First there is the contrast between normal weight and obese participants, known as the main effect of weight. This is indicated in Table 4.9.

Second, there is the contrast between the two levels of hunger, fed and starved. Do participants, on average, eat more cookies when they are hungry rather than satisfied. This second contrast is termed the main effect of hunger. This is indicated in Table 4.10.

Finally, the usual two-way ANOVA includes a test for the interaction of the two main effects. This tests whether the effect of one depends upon the other. For example, does the difference between being fed or starved depend on whether you consider participants who are obese or participants who have a normal weight? Put differently, is the difference between being fed or starved the same at each level of weight? The interaction term examines whether one predictor variable influences the effect of the other. If there is no significant interaction, then the two predictors are said to be independent of one another.

The design in this example is also a between subjects design. That is, each subject is tested under only one condition, and so different participants are used in each cell of the design. Imaginary data for a small number of fictitious participants is listed in Table 4.11.

Thus the contrasts made by the ANOVA are made between different subjects as well as between treatments. In a within subjects design, more

Table 4.10   Main effect of hunger

	Normal weight	Obese
↓ Recently fed	1	2
Starved	3	4

Table 4.11   Raw data for obesity study

	Normal weight	Obese
Recently fed	1, 2, 2,	5, 4, 3,
	2, 1, 1	5, 2, 4
Starved	4, 5, 5,	4, 4, 3,
	3, 5, 4	5, 2, 5

Table 4.12 Cell means for obesity study

	Normal weight	Obese
Recently fed	1.50	3.83
Starved	4.33	3.83

commonly called a repeated measures design, the same subjects are used in each cell. We will return to such designs in Chapter 7.

Each subject has a score, and we are going to use ANOVA to fit a model to these scores. The model for two-way ANOVA is:

M4.3: number of cookies eaten
= constant + weight + hunger + weight * hunger + error

The term *weight * hunger* represents the interaction of the two predictors. What this model says is that we believe we can, in part at least, account for the values of individual scores in terms of the influence of the two factors. Each score is determined, in part, by the effect of *weight*, the effect of *hunger* and the interaction of these two effects.

Table 4.12 shows the means for each group, and Table 4.13 shows the ANOVA for this fictitious data.

The ANOVA shows significant main effects of both *weight*, $F(1, 20) = 4.39$, $p < .05$, and *hunger*, $F(1, 20) = 11.23$, $p < .01$, but also a significant interaction between *weight* and *hunger* $F(1, 20) = 14.21$, $p < .01$. The significant interaction implies that the effect of *hunger* on the number of cookies eaten depends on which weight category a participant is from. To identify the effect, it is necessary to examine the cell means shown in Table 4.12. From these you can see that three cells have very similar means, but one cell has a lower mean. It appears that normal weight participants ate fewer cookies if they had been fed, but obese participants ate similar numbers of cookies irrespective of whether they had been fed or were starved. Schachter explained these results by suggesting that in normal weight participants, appetite is under the control of physiological hunger. Thus, normal weight people eat amounts of food that correspond to their nutritional requirements. The food intake of obese people, in contrast, is determined by external influences such as the laying of food before their eyes.

Table 4.13 Two-way analysis of obesity study

Source	SS	df	MS	F	p
Weight (W)	4.167	1	4.167	4.386	0.049
Hunger (H)	10.667	1	10.667	11.228	0.003
W × H	13.500	1	13.500	14.211	0.001
Error	19.000	20	0.950		

In this example, we have interpreted the interaction simply by inspecting the cell means. Normally, however, you would go one step further and check whether the differences (or absences of difference) can be confirmed statistically. This is done by directly comparing the cell means. This process is described in more detail in Chapter 8 which deals with testing specific hypotheses.

When there is more than one predictor variable in your model, ANOVA will test the interactions of predictors. If you find a significant interaction it will often have an important influence on your interpretation of your data. It is useful, therefore, to have a clear understanding of the concept of interaction.

Warrington and Weiskrantz (1970) investigated the performance of normal and amnesic subjects on two different memory tasks. The dependent variable is each participant's score on the memory task. The score for both tasks is the number of words correct. There are two predictor variables. The first is whether or not a participant is amnesic. The second is the distinction between the two memory tasks. The first task was a standard free recall test. Participants were presented with a list of words and subsequently had to recall them. The second task also involved presenting participants with a list of words, but this time the participant is merely required to identify the word. For example, the list they are presented with might include the word 'lamp'. They are subsequently shown words from the list briefly on a screen and they just have to identify it as the word 'lamp'. This second task is described as an implicit memory task because subjective awareness of remembering is not necessary for performance. Nevertheless, having seen the word in the initial presentation does assist performance, and so there does appear to be an influence of memory. The percentage of correct responses for each condition is shown in Table 4.14 and depicted in Fig. 4.4.

Warrington and Weiskrantz found a significant interaction between the two predictor variables. The results of this study suggest that although amnesic participants perform more poorly on the explicit memory task, on the implicit memory task they do as well as unimpaired participants. The impact of amnesia on performance depends on the particular memory task used. This distinction between implicit and explicit memory has influenced our understanding of the mechanisms underpinning memory in normal people.

Table 4.14 Memory performance of normal and amnesic subjects

	Normal	Amnesic
Implicit task	46%	48%
Recall	54%	33%

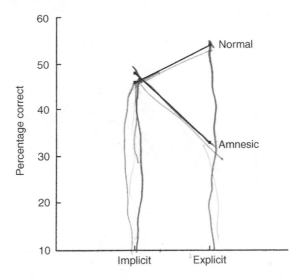

Figure 4.4 Memory performance for amnesic and control participants on two memory tasks

When there is no interaction between two predictor variables, they do not influence one another. The effect of each is independent of the other. In whatever way one variable is manipulated, the effect of the other is unchanged. Table 4.15 illustrates data with no interaction. The values shown are hypothetical cell means for the six combinations of two predictor variables. Predictor A has two levels, and predictor B has three levels. You can see that the difference between the levels of A, an indication of the effect of predictor A, is the same at every level of B. Each time, the difference between A1 and A2 is a change in mean score of + 3. You can see from Fig. 4.5 that when these means are plotted, the line for means at the first level of predictor A is parallel to the line for the second level. That is, the difference is constant. In a case where there is no interaction, the effect of one predictor is independent of manipulation of the other predictor. The response it produces is not influenced by changes in the other predictor. The effects of the two predictors are said to be additive.

Table 4.16 and Fig. 4.6, however, illustrate a case of interaction. In this example, the effect of A is not constant at every level of B. To know

Table 4.15 Additive relationship between explantory variables in two-way design

	B1	B2	B3
A1	1	5	6
A2	4	8	9

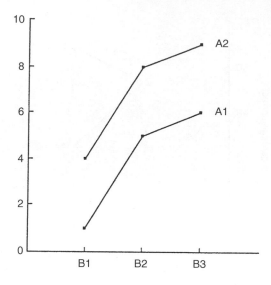

Figure 4.5 Additive relationship between two explanatory variables

the effect of A, you have to know the level of B. A has a larger effect at the third level of B than it does at the first level, for example. In fact, the mean at the second level of A is three times the corresponding value at the first level, as you can see from Table 4.16. The relationship between the two predictors is said to be multiplicative and there is an interaction. Figure 4.6 also shows that the lines are no longer parallel.

There are many examples in psychology of predictor variables that interact. For example, Broadbent (1971) established that the effects of noise and lack of sleep interact in certain tasks. Normally, when there is noise people perform more poorly. Similarly, someone who lacks sleep does not perform well. However, the performance of someone who lacks sleep is restored somewhat by the occurrence of noise. One theory of why this occurs is that both noise and sleep affect people's arousal. Lack of sleep diminishes arousal, while noise raises it. Performance is best when arousal is at an optimum level. Either too much or too little arousal leads to a deterioration in performance. However, people whose level of arousal is lowered through lack of sleep can, to some extent, have their arousal restored by noise. Thus, the effects of the two predictor variables

Table 4.16 Multiplicative relationship between explanatory variables in two-way design

	B1	B2	B3
A1	1	5	6
A2	3	15	18

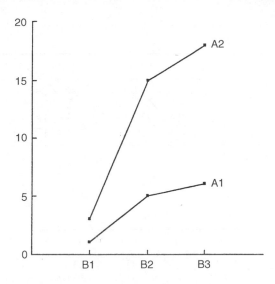

Figure 4.6 Multiplicative relationship between two explanatory variables

interact because they both influence the same psychological mechanism. Sternberg (1969) in an important paper argued that the absence of an interaction between two predictor variables was evidence that they did not influence a common psychological mechanism. Testing for interaction, he argued, could therefore be used to test hypotheses about the separation of psychological processes into distinct components.

When you carry out an ANOVA on data and find a significant interaction, it is necessary to reflect carefully on the interpretation of the result. It is appropriate, of course, to inspect the cell means so that you can see what the pattern of response is. You may also want to test whether specific differences between cell means are statistically significant, as discussed in Chapter 8. However, it is also possible for an interaction to arise just because of the way the data have been set out. You may find that by adjusting the way the data is described you can make what appears to be an interaction vanish.

Consider again the fictitious cell means given in Table 4.16. Imagine that the data come from an enlarged study of the relationship between skill and memory for board positions among chess players. In this enlarged study, there are three levels of skill: beginner (B1); inexperienced (B2); and expert (B3). Again, there are two levels of concurrent task: either there is no concurrent task (A2) or the concurrent task is for the participant to tap the points of a geometric figure cyclically (A1). This task is intended to occupy a component of working memory called the visuo-spatial sketchpad. Performance, let us imagine, is initially scored in terms of the number of pieces correctly positioned per minute (with each piece correct scoring a point and each piece incorrectly positioned losing a point as before), generating the means in Table 4.16. Raw data

Table 4.17 Artificial data exhibiting multiplicative relationship

	B1	B2	B3
A1	1, 1, 2, 1, 2, −1	5, 6, 7, 5, 4, 3	5, 7, 4, 8, 5, 7
A2	2, 3, 2 3, 4, 4	15, 17, 13, 17, 14, 14	18, 16, 20, 19, 17, 18

Table 4.18 Reciprocal transformation

	B1	B2	B3
A1	0.50	0.22	0.18
A2	0.36	0.07	0.06

for 36 imaginary participants conforming to this hypothetical outcome is presented in Table 4.17. This produces a significant interaction between concurrent task and skill as well as main effects of skill and concurrent task.

The interaction makes the interpretation of the main effects unclear. For example, although the concurrent task is linked with worse performance, it is not clear that this is so for all levels of player. Perhaps better players rely on the visuo-spatial sketchpad but novice players do not. However, if instead of scoring the task in terms of the number of pieces correctly positioned per minute, it is scored as the number of minutes taken on average to position one piece correctly, the results will be seen in a quite different light. This change in the manner of scoring is equivalent to a reciprocal transformation. For example, if a player positions five pieces correctly in a minute, then the number of minutes required to position each piece on average is 0.2. Means for the transformed data are shown in Table 4.18.

For this data, the interaction is not statistically significant, although both main effects still are. You may wish to verify this as an exercise. This example, it must be emphasized, is based on fictitious data. Nevertheless, it illustrates the general point that the way data is presented can influence the conclusions that are drawn from a study. Whether it is more appropriate to model the data using the number of minutes per piece or the number of pieces per minute will depend on the theoretical framework within which the phenomenon is understood. Frequently, however, interpretation will be clearer and conclusions will be drawn in a more straightforward way if there is no significant interaction term.

4.4 SUMMARY

ANOVA is usually employed when an investigator wants to know whether a predictor variable that has been manipulated has influenced a dependent variable. The investigator wants to know whether differences between scores at different levels of the independent variable are greater in magnitude than differences that might occur by chance. ANOVA permits the calculation of precise probabilities. These probabilities, or p-values, indicate how likely differences between levels are to have oc- curred if they were the product of nothing more than error variance.

ANOVA makes certain assumptions about the distribution of the data it is called upon to assess. When these assumptions are not met, the p-values calculated may not be precisely correct. It is appropriate to take steps to check whether the data you have does meet these assumptions or at least that it does not display features that grossly violate the assumptions.

ANOVA incorporating more than one predictor variable tests an interaction term. This term provides an assessment of whether the effect of each predictor is constant for all levels of other predictors in the model. If the interaction is significant then the effect of one predictor varies at different levels of another predictor. When the interaction is significant, careful consideration must be given to the interpretation of the results. Significant main effects in the same model must be interpreted in the light of the significant interaction. In addition, consideration must be given to the possibility that the appearance of an interaction is a function of the way the data has been coded. In any event, it is important to inspect the cell means to glean a picture of the pattern of results. In some cases this inspection will be followed up with specific comparisons to confirm that differences, or absences of difference, are statistically reliable.

5 MULTIPLE REGRESSION

Multiple regression is a procedure for fitting a model to data, where the model is a set of variables which you believe can explain, or predict, a score. For example, you might use it to relate the score on a test of reading ability to variables you think can help explain reading ability such as, say, age, picture-naming ability, socio-economic variables, birth-weight, time of day of testing and so on. You gather data for a sample of cases, recording the score of interest, reading ability, and the values of the predictor variables for each child. Multiple regression can then be used to attribute variation in reading ability to the different predictor variables, indicating which are most strongly associated with differences in reading ability.

Multiple regression has a number of advantages. You can use it to examine a large number of predictors simultaneously. You can do this with ANOVA, but with ANOVA you have to balance the cases you sample. As the number of predictor variables increases, this becomes cumbersome. For example, you would need the same number of 5 year-old rich kids with low birthweight tested in the morning and having moderate picture-naming scores as you had 7 year-old rich kids with high birthweight tested in the morning and having low picture-naming scores. And so on for each permutation of the predictors. It remains important to cover the range of possible cases, but for large numbers of predictors sampling is easier with multiple regression.

A second advantage is that multiple regression allows you to use more detailed information about the predictor variables. In ANOVA the predictor variables have to be categorical. That is, the values of the predictor variable have to be grouped into categories. For example, birthweight has to be converted into, say, high and low birthweight groups. However, underlying this dichotomy between the groups is a continuum of weights. When we group children into high versus low groups, information is lost about differences in weight among children within each group. Multiple regression allows you to retain this more precise information about predictor variables.

5.1   LINEAR REGRESSION

It is useful to begin with simple linear regression, which is used to predict the values of a score using one predictor variable. For example, Table 5.1 displays two scores for each of 10 subjects. The first score is a measure of reading ability, the second is a measure of parental income.

The correlation between these scores is .65. Figure 5.1 is a scatterplot of the data with the best-fitting straight line added.

The equation of the line is:

reading $= 9.1 + 0.37 *$ income

Table 5.1   Reading scores and parental income for ten fictitious children

Subject	Reading	Parental income
1	23	45 K
2	16	42 K
3	21	28 K
4	12	15 K
5	17	22 K
6	33	37 K
7	15	12 K
8	11	14 K
9	18	24 K
10	26	32 K

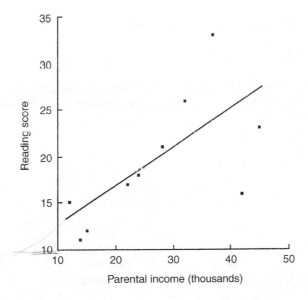

Figure 5.1   Relationship between parental income and reading score

Here, 9.1 is the point at which the line cuts the y-axis. In other words, it is the value of the y-variable when the x-variable is zero. In our example, it represents the predicted reading score of children whose parental income is nil. The value 0.37 is the gradient of the line. It is a measure of the steepness of the increase in reading scores as parental income increases. In our example, for every 1000 increase in income, reading scores are predicted to rise on average by 0.37 marks.

This equation allows you to relate values of the score (on the x-axis) to values of the predictor (reading scores). For example, if a new child joins the class we can use information about the income of that child's parents to predict the child's likely reading score. Say their income is 25 000, then the child's predicted reading score is:

$$\text{predicted score} = 9.1 + (0.37 * 25)$$
$$= 18.35$$

Let's try the same thing with one of the existing children. Take child 5, whose parental income is 22 000.

$$\text{predicted score} = 9.1 + (0.37 * 22)$$
$$= 17.24$$

This predicted score is a point on the best-fitting line. However, child 5's actual score, the score obtained when the child was tested, differs from this slightly. The difference between the obtained score and the predicted score is the residual:

$$\text{residual} = \text{obtained score} - \text{predicted score}$$
$$= 17 - 17.24$$
$$= -0.24$$

In general, the residual for any obtained score is the difference between it and the corresponding point on the best-fitting line. The residual for one data point is indicated in Fig. 5.2 by a vertical line. The length of the vertical line between the data point and the best fitting line corresponds to the size of the residual.

The line we have fitted here is known as the regression line, and the equation of the line is called the regression equation. The slope of line (B) is called the regression coefficient. We can relate this to our general equation:

$$\text{data} = \text{model} + \text{error}$$

Here, the model is the regression equation (constant + Bx)

$$\text{data} = \text{constant} + (B * \text{parental income}) + \text{residual}$$

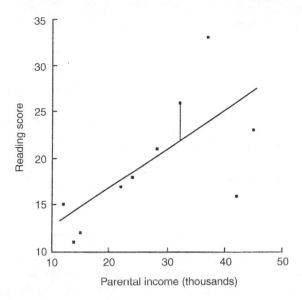

Figure 5.2   Residual for one child indicated by vertical line

Where: data is the obtained score
        constant is the *y*-intercept
        B is the regression coefficient
        residual is the difference between the predicted score and the
            obtained score

The predicted score is 9.1 + (0.37 ∗ parental income).

5.1.2 Linearity

Using linear regression assumes that the relationship between the score
and the predictor is linear. In other words, it assumes that, for example,
increasing parental income by a given amount always has the same effect
on reading scores. Increasing parental income by another 1K produces a
steady increase in reading score. In other words, we are assuming that
the best-fitting line really is a straight line. In some cases this is not so.
Consider the data in Table 5.2. For each subject, the first score is a
measure of exam performance, the second a measure of anxiety.

The scatterplot is shown in Fig. 5.3. A best-fitting straight line could be
fitted, but it should be clear that a curved line would provide a better fit
to the data. Although a straight line could be fitted to the data, we would
get a more accurate set of predictions from the curve. This data set
illustrates the Yerkes–Dodson curve relating anxiety to performance. The
original experiments were done with rats in the 1920s, but the results

Table 5.2 Exam performance and anxiety scores for ten fictitious subjects

Subject	Exam	Anxiety
1	5	56
2	4	118
3	5	124
4	3	42
5	6	72
6	6	105
7	8	90
8	8	95
9	7	102
10	7	88

have wide applicability. For example, athletes who get too 'psyched-up' before an event will actually perform less well. Increasing anxiety improves performance up to a point, but too much nervousness is a bad thing. Before a major event, when athletes will be naturally very anxious anyway, it can be useful to encourage relaxation exercises to decrease anxiety. When the best description of a relationship is not a straight line, linear regression (and multiple regression) are inappropriate. If you want to go ahead, either try to transform the variable so that the relationship is linear, or else consult an advanced text that explains how you can add a non-linear component to the model (e.g. Myers and Well, 1991).

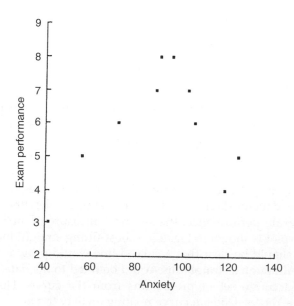

Figure 5.3 Relationship between anxiety and performance

5.1.3 Range of values in sample

When you use a regression equation to make predictions, you must be careful who you generalize the results to. For example, if the child of a rich merchant joins the class, does it really make sense to predict the reading score implied by a stratospheric income? The validity of the equation is really quite closely tied to the sample used to create the equation. It can be applied to new cases, but this is only appropriate if these new cases fall broadly in the range of values found in the original sample.

5.2 MULTIPLE REGRESSION

Multiple regression is just like simple linear regression, except that more than one predictor is included in the model. For example, you might want to predict reading scores using information about parental income and number of siblings. (Perhaps the more brothers and sisters a child has the better their reading scores?) The model will look like this:

reading score $=$ constant $+$ income $+$ siblings

The regression equation, once the model is fitted to the data, looks something like this (I have made up some brothers and sisters for this):

$$\text{reading score} = C + B1\text{income} + B2\text{siblings}$$
$$= 8.3 + 0.12 * \text{income} + 4.46 * \text{siblings}$$

Here, $B1$ and $B2$ are the regression coefficients for the two variables. If another new child joins the class (parental income $=$ 18K; two siblings), we estimate her reading score will be:

$$\text{score} = 8.3 + (0.12 * 18) + (4.46 * 2)$$
$$= 19.38$$

Again, there will be some error in the prediction. When the new child takes the reading test, her score will not be exactly the same as the estimate. Although the regression equation can be used to make predictions about new individual cases in this way, it is often useful just by letting you see the relative importance of different predictor variables. For example, you may want to model the influence of income on reading scores not to select children for school, but instead simply to understand the role and influence of different predictor variables.

5.2.1 Output

Table 5.3 displays the output of a typical statistics program for this multiple regression example (Systat 5). Applying multiple regression to a data set delivers a number of statistics. Most computer software prints these out automatically. The display shown above has three sections. The top part gives some overall statistics about the fit of the model to the data. The bottom part, headed Analysis of Variance, gives an overall test of the fit of the model. The middle part presents information about the role of each predictor in the model. The statistics for each predictor are shown in a row running across the page from the name of the predictor. However, your own statistics program will probably produce output that appears slightly different. The important thing is to understand what the key statistics are telling you about your model and the data.

The key part of the output consists of the regression coefficients for each predictor, together with the constant. These can be plugged into the regression equation. For each predictor, three other statistics are important. A *t*-test for each predictor (*T*) tests the null hypothesis that the regression coefficient for that predictor is not significantly different from zero. In other words, if this *t* is significant, the variable is making a useful contribution of its own to the prediction of the score. Second, the importance of different predictors can be compared using standardized

```
Regression

Dep var:READING    N:10    Multiple R: .852    Squared Multiple R: .725
Adjusted Squared Multiple R: .647       Standard Error of Estimate: 4.001

 Variable  Coefficient  Std Error   Std Coef  Tolerance     T     P(2 tail)

CONSTANT     8.330       3.332       0.000      .          2.500    0.041
  INCOME     0.121       0.145       0.212    0.6075741    0.833    0.432
    SIBS     4.464       1.615       0.703    0.6075741    2.764    0.028


                        Analysis of Variance

  Source    Sum-of-Squares   DF   Mean-Square    F-Ratio       P

Regression      295.557       2      147.778      9.233      0.011
  Residual      112.043       7       16.006
```

Table 5.3 Multiple regression output from the Systat computer software

regression coefficients. In the same way that standard scores let you compare tests based on different scales, standardized coefficients let you compare predictors based on different scales. Third, tolerance values indicate how closely related the predictors are to one another. If a given predictor variable correlates too highly with the others then, first, it is redundant and second, it can make the calculations involved in fitting the model to the data highly sensitive to small changes in the data. This results in regression coefficients that are unreliable. High values of tolerance indicate that a variable does not correlate too highly with the others. If the tolerance for a particular variable is less then about .1, then it may be sensible to omit that variable from the model and repeat the analysis without it.

It is useful to calculate and report a confidence interval for each regression coefficient that is significantly different from zero. First you need to get the critical value for the t-statistic from tables. Look up the critical value for the α-level corresponding to the desired confidence interval. For example, if you want a 95% confidence interval, look up the critical value for $\alpha = .05$, with $n - 2$ degrees of freedom (n = the number of subjects) in the table. With 10 subjects, the critical value for t with $\alpha = .05$ is 2.306. The upper limit of the confidence interval is then given by this formula:

upper limit = coefficient + (standard error of coefficient * critical value)

For example, the upper limit of the confidence interval for the siblings variable in the reading data example is:

$$
\begin{aligned}
\text{upper limit} &= 4.464 + (1.615 * 2.306) \\
&= 4.464 + 3.724 \\
&= 8.19
\end{aligned}
$$

Similarly, the lower limit is the coefficient − (standard error of coefficient * critical value). For this example, the lower limit is 0.74. You might check this as an exercise. Both the coefficient and its standard error are printed out by most computer software. Frequently, upper and lower 95% confidence limits are also printed out.

The multiple correlation (usually written R) is the correlation between the obtained scores and the scores predicted by the regression equation. It is a measure of the association between the predictors in the equation considered as a group and the score. The higher R is, the more closely the regression equation is predicting the score.

If you square a correlation coefficient, you get an estimate of the amount of variance accounted for. For example, if an attitude questionnaire correlates $r = .9$ with voting behaviour, then 81% of variation in voting behaviour can be accounted for by the attitude questionnaire. In multiple regression, R^2, the squared multiple correlation, is the proportion of the variance in the score that the predictors in the model can account for.

An ANOVA is usually printed out by computer software. This ANOVA table tests whether the ability of the whole set of predictor variables to predict the score is statistically significant. Literally, it tests whether the regression coefficients for the predictors differ from zero. If the F-ratio is not significant, then the null hypothesis (that the regression coefficients are zero) cannot be rejected.

5.3 WHAT THE REGRESSION COEFFICIENTS MEAN

A regression coefficient estimates the marginal effect of a variable — that is, the influence of that variable on the outcome (the predictor, the score) when all other variables in the model are held constant. For example, the coefficient for parental income in this equation indicates that if the number of siblings is held constant, then increasing parental income by 1K on average leads to a 0.37 increase in reading score.

However, it is important to bear in mind that the regression model does not in itself imply a causal relationship between the predictor variables and the outcome. Significant regression coefficients indicate significant associations between the predictors and the outcome. Inferences about causality depend on the design of your study rather than the statistical analysis. Only if you have manipulated the predictors with randomly assigned groups of subjects can you begin to make inferences about cause and effect relations.

Indeed, even if there is a direct causal relationship between, say, parental income and reading ability scores, it can be too simple to talk of 1K rises in salary producing 0.37 points increases in reading scores given that number of siblings is constant. It may not, in the real world, be the case that number of siblings can be held constant as parental income rises. For example, it may be that increases in parental income also cause changes in the number of children a family has. In this case parental income not only has a direct effect on reading scores, but an indirect one too. Parental income influences number of siblings and through that indirectly influences reading ability in a second way. Variables can have both direct and indirect effects on outcomes.

You also need to be aware that the size of regression coefficients and their significance level depend on which other variables are included in the model. Imagine that we are trying to predict how successful a hockey team will be. Assume that really and truly there are three factors determining success: accuracy of passing, skill at tackling and physical fitness. Assume also that these factors are independent: they are not correlated with one another. However, as researchers, we do not know any of this yet and we try to build our model using the following predictor variables which we believe are relevant:

1. height:weight ratio of players;
2. rate of success on penalty corners;
3. speed of players;
4. average number of passes in own moves.

We would find that all of these played some role as predictors. The first and third pick up some of the variance that is really due to fitness. The second and fourth are associated with the success of the team because they reflect passing skill. However, these pairs have to share the variance of the relevant factor. For example, 'penalties' and 'number of passes' share the variance that is actually caused by variation in passing skill. If we constructed the model with only the first three variables (i.e. missing out 'number of passes'), then 'penalties' would have a higher regression coefficient because it would be getting the passing skill variance all to itself.

When the effects of two predictors are closely related like this, they affect each other's regression coefficients. In the hockey example, the predictor variables partially overlap. If any variable is completely redundant, so that its effects actually overlap completely with the effects of other variables in the model, then the analysis is jeopardized and you need to get rid of the redundant variable. This situation is called multicollinearity and arises when a predictor variable is a linear function of the other predictors. In this situation, the regression coefficients are intolerably unstable, and can change dramatically if only a few outcomes change. In other words, if you changed a small number of scores on the predictor, you could find a large change in the regression coefficients resulting. You can detect multicollinearity by looking at the tolerance values in the computer software output. When a variable has high tolerance it is more independent of the other predictors. That is, there is a low correlation between that variable and other predictor variables. If tolerance drops below .1, then you need to consider jettisoning the variable from your model.

5.4 SAMPLE SIZE AND CROSS-VALIDATION

If the sample used to estimate the regression coefficients is too small, the regression equation will not generalize very well to new samples. When the sample is small, the coefficients estimated owe too much to the idiosyncracies and peculiarities of the sample. The coefficients depend too heavily on the particular cases included in the sample. Tabachnik and Fidell (1989, p.128) offer the following rules of thumb for choosing sample size. 'As a bare minimum requirement ... have at least 5 times more cases than [predictor variables] — at least 25 cases if 5 [predictors] are used. However, one would like to have 20 times more cases than [predictors].'

A check on the reliability of a regression equation can be made using cross-validation. Ideally, this is done by collecting a fresh sample of data from new subjects. In a large scale project, you would do that, but often you will not have the resources. However, cross-validation can be carried out using only your original sample. This is sometimes called jack-knifing. The equation is constructed using only 80% of the cases observed. The resulting equation is then used to predict values for the other 20% of cases. The correlation between predicted values and obtained values for the 20% subset is squared to give a second estimate of R^2. If this is very different from the original R^2 obtained from the 80% group when the regression equation was constructed, then there is a problem with the regression equation. If the new R^2 is markedly different, then the coefficients in the equation are not producing good generalization. One way to deal with this problem is to reduce the number of predictor variables in the model. If there are too many predictors for the sample size, then generalization can be poor.

5.5   STEPWISE REGRESSION

In standard multiple regression, you try all the predictor variables you are considering in the model. All of these predictors are put in the model at the start. However, as we have seen, the sizes of the regression coefficients can depend on which other predictors are in the model. Because predictors can be correlated with each other as well as with the outcome score, they can affect one another's regression coefficients. This leads to a tactical dilemma: of all the potential predictors you have data for, which should be included in the model? In the hockey example above, we saw that four predictors in the model were covering the effects of two real causal influences (and a third causal influence was not represented in the model at all). How is the researcher to decide, in necessary ignorance of the identity of the true causes, which of the four to include in the model? One approach is to fit your model in a series of steps, adding one further predictor to the model at a time. Predictors are only kept if they significantly improve the fit of the regression equation. Predictors are added in an order that reflects their importance, so that the most important are added first, untrammelled by less important ones. You need criteria for deciding which predictors are the most important. The criteria can be purely statistical (size of improvement of R^2, for instance) or they can reflect your own theoretical appreciation of the problem being studied. In the latter case, the method is known as hierarchical regression. Hierarchical regression is discussed in detail in Chapter 9.

With stepwise regression, you have to be very cautious about the interpretation of probability values, especially where the selection of predictors is *post hoc* or statistically based. Because you have been fishing around for the model that fits best, you really are open to bias that results from the problem of multiplicity (see Chapter 2). The choice of predictors to include in the model deserves careful reflection and attention to diagnostic statistics such as tolerance values.

5.6 REGRESSION AND CORRELATION

There is a close relationship between regression coefficients and correlation coefficients. If the two variables have the same standard deviation, then the correlation coefficient is exactly the same as the regression coefficient in simple linear regression. This can be illustrated using the data on reading ability from above. The regression coefficient is .37, the correlation coefficient is .65. However, if the variables are given the same standard deviation, for example by converting them to standard scores, and then a regression line is fitted to these transformed scores, the regression coefficient matches the correlation. You can check this using the standardized scores for the reading ability data given in Table 5.4.

The correlation is the same whether scores are standardized or not ($r = .652$). When the scores are standardized, the regression coefficient is also .652. The standardized coefficient mentioned above is the regression coefficient that would be obtained from standardized data. Perhaps counterintuitively, this standardized regression coefficient is less useful than the ordinary one for the application of the model to new data. If you want to apply the reading scores equation to a new group of children to compute predictions, the original coefficients are more likely to be

Table 5.4 Standardized reading scores and parental income

Subject	Reading	Income	Reading standard scores	Income standard scores
1	23	45 000	0.565	1.521
2	16	42 000	−0.476	1.266
3	21	28 000	0.267	0.076
4	12	15 000	−1.070	−1.028
5	17	22 000	−0.327	−0.433
6	33	37 000	2.051	0.841
7	15	12 000	−0.624	−1.283
8	11	14 000	−1.218	−1.113
9	18	24 000	−0.178	−0.263
10	26	32 000	1.010	0.416

accurate than the standardized ones. However, the standardized coefficients are useful for comparing the relative importance of predictors.

5.7   MULTIPLE REGRESSION AND ANOVA

You can think of ANOVA as a special case of multiple regression in which all of the predictor variables, called factors in ANOVA, are categorical. For example, in Schachter's experiment on obesity, which we discussed in Chapter 4, the predictors were hunger and weight, and these variables were split into categories (obese versus normal, and so on). When the values on all the predictors are grouped into categories (levels), multiple regression and ANOVA are identical. Multiple regression can deal with most things ANOVA can — and more. In fact, both ANOVA and multiple regression are instances of the general linear model.

5.8   ASSUMPTIONS OF MULTIPLE REGRESSION

Checking assumptions is detailed in Chapter 3, on data screening and data repair. In multiple regression, data need to be checked for missing values and outliers as discussed earlier. In addition there are five specific assumptions of multiple regression.

1. there is no multicollinearity;
2. the residuals are normally distributed, with a mean of zero;
3. the variance of residuals is the same throughout the range of scores on the predicted variable;
4. the scores on the variable being predicted are independent of each other;
5. relationships between predictors and the outcome variable are linear.

To check these assumptions:

1. check that no tolerance values are less than 0.1;
2. (a) plot the residuals (e.g. stem and leaf or normal probability plot) and check for a broadly normal distribution, (b) plot residuals against estimates (scatterplot) and check the distribution;
3. plot the residuals against estimates (scatterplot) and check that the spread of residuals is similar throughout the range of estimates;
4. sometimes, for example, there is an effect of the order in which subjects were tested: plot residuals against order of cases — there should be no distinctive pattern or cycle;

5. draw scatterplots to show the relationship between each predictor variable and the score being predicted.

In addition, multiple regression can be affected by multivariate outliers. A multivariate outlier arises when a subject has an unusual combination of scores on different predictors. For example, suppose you are interested in the development of literacy skills. A sample of the normal school population might be tested on reading comprehension and given a short spelling test. These two variables will tend to be correlated, so that children who do well on one also do well on the other. Imagine, however, that one child gets a standard score of 0.8 on the reading test, indicating that their understanding is above average, but -1.3 on the spelling test (see Chapter 11 for an explanation of standard scores). This is an unusual combination of scores. You would want to follow this up, and possibly consider deleting this child's data from the study. For example, perhaps they have a specific learning disorder. In that case, they would not be a member of the population you were trying to sample, and you would not necessarily expect a model of normal reading skills to fit them. Many statistics packages provide a value called the Mahalanobis distance for each subject. If the Mahalanobis distance is large, that subject is a multivariate outlier.

5.9 SUMMARY

Multiple regression lets you model scores using a number of predictors. You can use it where you have scores for a number of cases or individuals and you have recorded values on the predictor variables for each case. You can test the overall fit of the model and the individual predictor variables. The results can be used to create a regression equation which can predict scores for new cases, although often this is not required.

Interpretation of multiple regression relies on careful consideration of whether the assumptions of the test have been met, the appropriateness of the sample of data used and the design of the study that produced the data.

6 MORE EXPLORATORY DATA ANALYSIS

In the chapter on data screening, we looked at residual scores as a source of further information about the data. In the first section of this chapter, that idea is developed in greater detail. We look first at a relatively simple example in which we search for a pattern in the residuals using graphical methods. A second example introduces the analysis of covariance as an exploratory technique. Exploratory data analysis of this kind is not used to test hypotheses in the usual way. Rather, it is used to help reveal avenues along which further research might fruitfully be directed. The second section of the chapter looks at methods suitable for the exploration of multivariate data sets.

6.1 EXPLORING RESIDUALS

Think of your data as a mug of coffee. When you drink the coffee, there is something left over at the bottom of the mug. This left over portion is the residue. When you fit a model to data, the statistical analysis extracts as much pattern from the data as it can. Variation which the model cannot account for is the residual variance. This is the variance remaining when all the variance attributable to the explanatory variables in the model is taken away.

An assumption of parametric statistical tests is that this residual variance, or error variance, represents the effect only of random error. However, if a variable that was not included in the model had a systematic effect on scores, then its influence can sometimes be detected in the residuals. If there is evidence of a systematic pattern in the residual scores, then that can be linked to the influence of a variable that was not included in your original model. When you reveal a pattern in the residuals, you have evidence that an additional variable may be needed to account for the results.

One way to demonstrate the existence of a pattern in the residuals is simply to plot them against variables that were not included in your model. A scatterplot will reveal whether there is any hint of a systematic relationship. If there is no relationship, points will be scattered uniformly across the plot. If there is a relationship, then the points will form a pattern.

Here is a fictitious example. A researcher tests a group of students to evaluate whether good chess players have a better memory for board layouts than weak players. A chess board is set out with pieces arranged in a way that conforms to the rules of chess. Subjects are tested individually. Each subject sees the board for one minute. The board is then covered. The subject must then position pieces from another set on an empty board. Their score is the number of pieces positioned correctly. Table 6.1 contains fictitious raw data for the two groups.

A one-way ANOVA shows that the difference between these groups is statistically significant, $F(1, 12) = 10.96$, $p < .01$. However, in Table 6.2 I give two further pieces of information. In the first new column, the residual score for each case is given. In the second, the time of day at which the subject was tested is given.

Table 6.1 Number of pieces correctly positioned

Weak players	Good players
12	14
8	13
15	18
11	16
9	16
12	21
15	17

Table 6.2 Residuals and time of day tested

Weak players		Strong players	
Time	Residual	Time	Residual
1100	0.286	1400	−2.429
1400	−3.714	1500	−3.429
1000	3.286	1100	1.571
1200	0.714	1000	−0.429
1500	−2.714	1000	−0.429
1000	0.286	1100	4.571
1200	3.286	1200	0.571

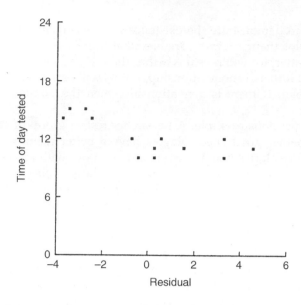

Figure 6.1 Relationship between time of day and residuals

Figure 6.1 plots the relationship betwen time of day of testing and residual scores on the test. As you can see, there is a weak relationship. This suggests that time of day influences scores.

When you find a pattern in residuals, you attempt to generate an account that explains the pattern. This process of considering possible explanations is inevitably speculative. You are generating new hypotheses. The study you did was not designed to test these hypotheses, and you are unlikely to have data that can determine conclusively whether they are correct. What you can do is highlight issues that should be considered in further research. For example, you might decide to design a study that investigates time of day effects on memory performance. Alternatively, you might determine that in future studies you will control the order in which groups are tested, or that you will stick to a single uniform set of instructions throughout the study, in case variation might affect results.

6.2 ANALYSIS OF COVARIANCE

We move now to an example that is statistically more sophisticated. Nonetheless, the same basic idea is used: you can discover something new by looking for patterns in the residuals. The residuals are the unexplained variance in a data set. If we find a pattern in the residuals, we may use it to help us develop an explanation for some of this residual variance. Any pattern in the residuals is a clue that can help us

Table 6.3 Mean performance in noise

Low noise	Medium noise	High noise
4.43	7.57	6.71

understand the phenomenon under investigation. The following example uses analysis of covariance to reduce error variance.

Imagine an experiment investigating the effect of noise on cognitive performance. We start with three conditions: high, medium and low noise. In each condition subjects tackle a simple arithmetic task. The dependent variable is their score on this task. The model here is shown as M:6.1.

M6.1: score = noise + error

We predict there will be differences in the performance of subjects in these three conditions. Specifically, we expect performance to be worse when the noise level is high. After gathering the data, we begin with simple descriptive statistics. Table 6.3 gives the means for the three groups (i.e. the three levels of the variable noise).

This suggests our hypothesis was at least partly correct. Let's assume we have chosen the statistical test to use for assessing the significance of these means: one-way ANOVA. The α-level will be .05, and the null hypothesis is of no difference between the means. In Chapter 8 we will examine ways of testing the more specific hypothesis that the mean scores fall as the noise gets louder; at the moment we are just testing whether performance changes at all as the noise increases. Table 6.4 displays the ANOVA for these data.

Let's say, however, that we look at this data and consider whether there is something we have not taken into account that is systematically affecting scores. For example, what about the basic ability of each subject at the task? Presumably subjects' scores were influenced by their initial competence in arithmetic. Subjects better at arithmetic will have better scores. Perhaps if we draw out this variable, we can improve our understanding of the phenomenon. If the variance of subjects' scores is to some extent controlled by their natural ability, then it might be worthwhile taking this ability into account in our model. We have relied on the random assignment of subjects to conditions to even things out

Table 6.4 One-way analysis of performance data

Source	SS	df	MS	F	p
Noise	36.952	2	18.476	12.383	0.001
Error	26.857	18	1.492		

between the groups. We assume that equal numbers of subjects good at arithmetic end up in the three groups, and that no particular group is having its mean lowered purely by the presence of more than its fair share of poor counters. However, it may be that, if we took account of the baseline advantage of some subjects and evened things by mopping up variance explained by baseline skill, perhaps the effect of noise would stand out more clearly.

There is a technique you can use. Analysis of covariance allows you to subtract from subjects' scores any differences due to some external variable. The external variable — in our example, baseline ability — is called the covariate. Analysis of covariance allows you to test whether there are significant differences between the three noise level groups after taking into account any differences in baseline ability.

Analysis of covariance subtracts the effect of the covariate. The relationship between the covariate and the dependent variable is taken out, and the contrast between experimental treatments is made using only the variance that is left after the effect of the covariate has been removed. Figure 6.2 shows the relationship between the covariate and the outcome variable for our example. The regression line summarizes the extent to which the covariate itself can account for the scores.

We can model the performance scores in terms of the covariate as follows:

performance score = covariate + residual

From this perspective, the residual is a measure of everything apart from the covariate that affects performance. This residual includes the effect of differences in noise level and error variance. It is what is left after you remove the effect of prior skill. In Fig. 6.2, one of the points has been highlighted. The vertical line from this point to the regression line shows the residual for the point. This is the difference between the highlighted point, an actual score, and the score predicted by the covariate, the corresponding point on the line.

This difference represents an adjusted score: the actual score minus the effect of the covariate. If we could do our analysis on these residual scores instead of the raw data, we could test the hypothesis about noise with data from which effects of the covariate have been removed. Analysis of covariance calculates the regression of the covariate on the dependent variable and subtracts this effect from each score. Thus:

adjusted score = performance score − covariate

This adjusted score is simply the residual. It evens things up. The ordinary ANOVA is then carried out using the adjusted scores. This is a useful way to conceptualize what analysis of covariance does. The adjusted scores estimate performance assuming that everybody had

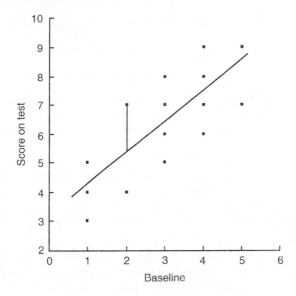

Figure 6.2 Residual following regression of baseline against test score indicated by vertical line

the same value for the covariate. In our example, it puts the analysis on the basis that all subjects start out with the same prior ability in arithmetic.

The model for analysis of covariance is shown in M6.2. The corresponding ANOVA was shown in M6.1. The difference between the models is that analysis of covariance draws out a component of error variance and provides an explicit term for it. This leads to a reduction in the size of the error term and thus to a more powerful test of the treatment effect. The analysis of covariance model has no interaction term. One of the assumptions of analysis of covariance is that the effect of the covariate is the same at all levels of the variable in the experiment. In other words, analysis of covariance assumes no interaction between noise and baseline. We will see how this assumption can be checked shortly.

M6.2: performance = noise + baseline + error

The analysis of covariance is shown in Table 6.5. Compared with the original one-way ANOVA we did above, the *F*-ratio for the treatment effect is slightly higher, mainly because the error variance has been halved. The covariate has mopped up a fair bit of the error variance.

The procedure for calculating analysis of covariance does not involve any calculations you have not previously covered. It involves some calculations similar to those used to work out a correlation, and some calculations like those used in ANOVA. Analysis of covariance can also

Table 6.5 Analysis of covariance of performance data with baseline

Source	SS	df	MS	F	p
Noise	16.932	2	8.466	13.970	0.001
Baseline	16.555	1	16.555	27.319	0.001
Error	10.302	17	0.606		

be used when there is more than one factor or when there is more than one covariate. The basic idea and the basic calculations do not change. However, the process of calculating analysis of covariance is tedious and only marginally edifying. If you feel like following through calculations in detail, either Ferguson (1981) or Winer (1971) provides a thorough treatment. Myers and Well (1991) provides a more accessible account.

One important assumption of analysis of covariance is that the co-variate covaries with the dependent variable in the same way at all levels of the treatment effect. If, for example, prior skill influences performance only at the highest noise levels, then analysis of covariance is not appropriate. For example, it might happen that weaker mathematicians are affected both by medium and high noise. If more skilful counters show no decrease in performance at medium noise levels but are only affected by high noise, then prior ability interacts with the effect of noise. Increases in noise would then not have parallel effects on weak and strong counters. Technically, analysis of covariance assumes that the regression lines predicting performance (the dependent variable) from baseline ability (the covariate) have the same slope for each level of noise. Figure 6.3 shows the relationship between the covariate and the dependent variable separately for each level of the independent variable. The homogeneity of slopes assumption is that the separate regression lines drawn for each level of the independent variable will be parallel to one another.

Whether the regression lines conform adequately to this assumption is checked by testing the model M6.3.

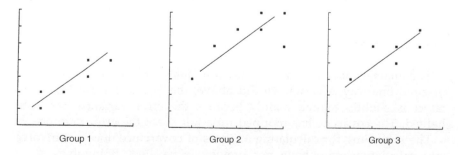

Group 1   Group 2   Group 3

Figure 6.3 Homogeneity of the slope of the regression of baseline against test score across the three groups

Table 6.6 Analysis testing homogeneity of slopes assumption

Source	SS	df	MS	F	p
Noise (N)	6.693	2	3.346	5.210	0.019
Baseline (B)	15.672	1	15.672	24.399	0.001
N × B	0.667	2	0.334	0.519	0.605
Error	9.635	15	0.642		

M6.3: performance = noise + baseline + noise ∗ baseline + error

We are looking for a non-significant interaction term, which we clearly get (Table 6.6). This indicates that the effect of the covariate is similar for all levels of noise, and so the homogeneity of slopes assumption is met. Remember that you must check that there is no interaction between the covariate and the independent variable if you use analysis of covariance.

Analysis of covariance is useful as a way of taking into account the influence of a variable which you find has a systematic effect on the outcome. It allows a model to be constructed which allows for this influence when the main hypothesis is tested. I have emphasized this as a technique to be used when the influence of the covariate has emerged as a result of model adequacy checking. In this case, the experimenter has relied on the random assignment of subjects to treatments to balance out the influence of extraneous variables. However, it becomes clear that it would be useful to make an explicit statistical allowance for the variable. This is an appropriate use of analysis of covariance and can result in more powerful tests of hypotheses.

An alternative way of getting round the reliance on random assign-ment of subjects to conditions would be to run the experiment again, but design it as a two-way ANOVA. We still have the variable loudness of noise with three levels. However, we add in a new variable — arithmetic baseline. This might have, say, two levels (weak or strong). We could use subjects' scores in an arithmetic test to assign them to groups. This new variable would mean our model is this:

M6.4: score = constant + noise + baseline + noise ∗ baseline + error

In M6.4, variance due to baseline ability is going to get attributed to the variable *baseline* and so will not mask the effects associated with the factor *noise*. Note that M6.4 includes an interaction term, which can be very useful. The difference between M6.4 and M6.3 is that M6.4 is being applied to a designed two factor experiment and so the interaction can be tested, while M6.3 is being applied just to check for the absence of interaction in a situation where the lack of balance in the design prevents a full test of the interaction. Obviously, you can only be in a position to do this if you anticipate the influence of the covariate before running the experiment. Indeed, when you find an important covariate through model adequacy checking this may lead you to design a new study which incorporates this new variable in the design.

It is possible, but inappropriate, to construct a factorial design like this in a *post hoc* way. This would involve constructing a categorical variable using scores on the covariate. Subjects would be divided into groups of weak and strong mathematicians after the influence of this variable had emerged without running a new study. M6.4 would be applied to the reorganized data. This will almost certainly lead to an unbalanced design because it is unlikely that exactly the same number of subjects in each condition will be good or bad at arithmetic. Furthermore, the F-tests that result will be biased. When the influence of a variable becomes clear during model adequacy checking, you can carry out an analysis of covariance, but it would be incorrect to confect a factorial design by reorganizing the data you have gathered.

However, it is legitimate to use analysis of covariance to allow for the effect of a variable even when you were able to anticipate its influence in advance. That is, instead of incorporating the variable as a factor in the design, you record it and control it statistically using analysis of covariance. This might be preferred when an investigator is not really interested in testing hypotheses about the covariate, but does want to control for its influence. In these circumstances, you can use scores on the covariate to assign subjects to treatments. That is, you assign subjects to treatments so that the average standing of subjects in terms of their score on the covariate is the same within each group. This effectively combines statistical and experimental control. In certain circumstances, this can be more powerful than developing a complete factorial design (Maxwell *et al*, 1984).

Analysis of covariance is sometimes used to apply a statistical correction to the scores of two groups which inherently differ on some variable. For example, you might be comparing children's performance under two different teaching regimes (say, boarding school versus day school). However, you recognize that the two groups differ systematically in terms of parental income. Concerned that this might contaminate the test of your central hypothesis about teaching regimes, you employ analysis of covariance to apply a statistical equalization of wealth. Analysis of covariance will mechanically do this, but you need to be aware that the resulting F-tests are biased. Furthermore, the interpretation of the results will be difficult for exactly the same reasons that the findings of any quasi-experimental study are ambiguous. There may be other differences between the groups than the ones you have identified, and because they are confounded with those you include explicitly in the statistical analysis, their influence cannot be discriminated. Random assignment of subjects to teaching methods would be necesary to license unambiguous inferences.

6.3 ASSUMPTIONS OF ANALYSIS OF COVARIANCE

Analysis of covariance makes the same asumptions as ANOVA, and three specific additional assumptions. A checklist of these is provided in this section for reference.

1. *Homogeneity of slopes* — check there is no interaction between the covariate and the treatment.
2. *Comparability of covariate scores* — check that the covariate scores are distributed roughly in a similar way for each level of the independent variable.
3. *Linearity of slopes* — the regression line fitted that relates the covariate to the dependent variable should be straight.

In addition, it should be noted that analysis of covariance requires careful interpretation. The same problems that affect the interpretation of correlations affect the interpretation of analysis of covariance. What we have found is nothing more than an association. We have not established a causal link. All we have is a pattern in the data.

Patterns uncovered by EDA need to be pursued in further research. Finding an association is not enough. We must follow up with designed experiments to establish a causal link. We have to be careful with analysis of covariance. If you know in advance that you want to control for the covariate, do it in the design so that you can use a two-way ANOVA, for instance. Covariance is useful on those occasions when hindsight performs better than foresight.

This section has looked in further detail at the role of EDA in uncovering patterns in data. We have also discussed weaknesses in EDA that stem from its essentially after-the-event character. In the next section, we will look at several exploratory techniques that can be applied to multivariate data.

6.4 EXPLORATORY MULTIVARIATE DATA ANALYSIS

It is increasingly common for studies in the behavioural sciences to examine a number of variables associated with a phenomenon at the same time. It is a truism that psychological phenomena tend to be complex and influenced by many things. For example, the performance of a child in school examinations may be influenced by their ability in the subject, their reading speed, the quality of their teacher, the method of teaching, their parents' educational attainment, their socio-economic background. The list could be extended easily. Researchers naturally want to incorporate relevant influences into their analysis. As resources for computing have become available, techniques to facilitate the analysis of multivariate data have been developed and psychologists have acquired the means to apply these techniques.

This section of the chapter describes a small number of methods which can help you to detect regularities or patterns in multivariate data. Familiar techniques, such as the scatterplot, are of limited usefulness because they only show two variables at a time. For example, you could plot examination score against parental income, but this would not convey any information about other variables you had recorded. What is needed is a technique that displays scores for several variables together on a single plot.

A simple way of depicting the relationships among several variables at once is to draw a series of bivariate plots, one for each pair of variables, and then to display all these plots together in a single figure. The different plots can then be compared by eye. A small example is displayed in Fig. 6.4 for some imaginary data for young offenders. This is called a scatterplot matrix, and can be useful in highlighting general features of relationships among variables. For example, a scatterplot matrix makes readily apparent the presence of any non-linear relationship. However, it also has limitations. First, it displays only pairwise relationships among variables. And second, it does not facilitate the identification of groups of cases which are similar, such as, say, children with low IQ scores and poor social adjustment who have poor records.

The variables used in this and the next two figures are record (an indication of the number of offences committed), adjusted (a measure of social adjustment), IQ (a measure of intelligence), sport (an indication of the offender's enthusiasm for contact sports), and, in Fig. 6.6 only, movies (a measure of interest in pornographic video material). In Fig. 6.4, 100 imaginary cases are plotted, but in Fig. 6.5 and 6.6 only four are displayed.

Chernoff (1973) introduced a technique for representing multivariate data based on the human face. People are good at seeing faces, and they find it relatively easy to relate to information conveyed in this form. An individual case is plotted as a line-drawing of a face. Each feature of the face corresponds to one variable. For example, scores on the IQ test might be represented by the shape of the mouth (good scores are bigger smiles). Figure 6.5 shows the same fictional data plotted as Chernoff faces. This kind of plot can be helpful in indicating what kinds of grouping there are among cases and revealing patterns of scoring across several variables.

An elegant technique for presenting multivariate data was developed by Andrews (1972) who suggested that a harmonic function with the following form should be used:

$$fx(t) = X_1/\sqrt{2} + X_2\sin t + X_3\cos t + X_4\sin 2t + X_5\cos 2t + X_6\sin 3t + \ldots\,\dot{}$$

X_n is the data value for a particular case on the nth variable. A point is calculated using values of t in the range $+/-\pi$, and these points are connected to create the curve for this case. The x-coordinate of the point is the value of t. The y-coordinate is calculated using the function. A separate curve is plotted for each case using this function. For example, assume we have one subject, called Bob. He scores 0.7, 0.5 and 0.8 on three measures ($X_1 = X_3$ respectively). The y-coordinate of the first point is calculated as:

$$X_1/\sqrt{2} + X_2\sin t + X_3\cos t = 0.7/\sqrt{2} + (0.5 * \sin\pi) + (0.8 * \cos\pi)$$
$$= z$$

This point is therefore plotted as (π, z). Of course, this is not done by hand. du Toit, Steyn and Stumpf (1986) discuss this procedure and the others described in this section. Andrews curves for our fictional offenders are shown in Fig. 6.6. The curve for the fourth offender, whose

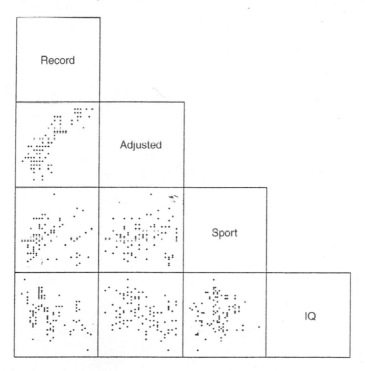

Figure 6.4   Scatterplot matrix for data from 100 fictitious young offenders

Figure 6.5   Chernoff faces for four young offenders

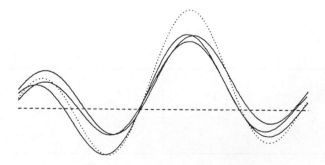

Figure 6.6   Andrews curves for four young offenders

Chernoff face appears at the bottom right of Fig. 6.5, has been drawn with a dotted line.

6.5 PRINCIPAL COMPONENTS ANALYSIS

An alternative to trying to see the effects of several variables simultaneously with a plot is to reduce the number of variables. There are different ways to do this. One relatively straightforward course of action would be to manually select a small number of variables for further examination. For example, you might select a measure of IQ and another measure of parental income as variables for scrutiny. Parental income would represent, say, social influences. IQ would stand for various measures of ability. To the extent that each was representative of distinct and important dimensions of variation, they would carry the information contained in other variables. That is, if other measures related to social influence did correlate with parental income then parental income could stand for them. And if measures such as reading speed or vocabulary did correlate with IQ then it would be a good representative. You could proceed with the analysis using just IQ and parental income as predictor variables.

Often, however, you will be reluctant to straightforwardly discard variables you have taken trouble to record. Selecting just one variable as a representative will preserve only variance shared with that variable. To the extent that it does not correlate with other variables it is chosen to represent, it will not carry information about them.

Principal components analysis (PCA) offers a way to boil down a set of variables into a small number of variables that account for as much of the variance in the original variables as possible. It is easiest to explain with an example. Imagine you are studying a sample of scrambled egg. An egg has been cracked and dropped into some cool but melted butter where the motion of a wooden spoon has gently stirred it. It has begun to cook. At this point, you gather some samples of the mixture. You test each sample in various ways. In particular, you record the colour saturation, the percentage content of palmitic acid, vitamin D and albumin content for each sample. Fictitious data for 10 imaginary samples is displayed in Table 6.7. The scores of different samples on each variable are correlated. For example, samples which are more yellow tend to have higher palmitic acid content. Principal components analysis extracts regularities in the pattern of correlations. The principal components of scrambled egg, let us agree, are the white and the yolk. A good analysis will distinguish these components.

Table 6.8 displays the results of PCA performed on the data in Table 6.7. The first two components are shown. The first component accounts for 64% of the total variation in scores. Each component is a synthetic

Table 6.7 Scrambled egg

Yellowness	Palmitic acid	Vitamin D	Albumin
11	9	0.10	21.4
14	12	0.40	12.6
10	8	0.05	14.0
12	11	0.20	18.6
15	13	0.15	17.0
10	8	0.20	21.0
12	9	0.15	14.0
14	12	0.30	21.2
15	13	0.25	14.6
11	9	0.10	18.2

variable created by the analysis which stands as a summary for a subset of the original variables. Principal components analysis reduces a large set of observed variables to a small number of principal components. The loadings show the correlation between each of the original variables and the different principal components. For example, scores on the palmitic acid variable correlate 0.949 with scores on the first principal component. Each component is interpreted by examining which of the original variables loads highly on it. The first component has high loadings for yellowness, palmitic acid and vitamin D content. In fact, vitamin D is found in egg yolk, and palmitic acid is a saturated fat found in both egg yolk and butter. The first component (PC1) appears to correspond to a yolk component. PC2 has a high loading only for albumin, which is a constituent of egg white and which gives it the properties so greatly admired by those who enjoy meringue.

Principal components analysis is an exploratory technique that can reduce a large number of variables to a small number of key dimensions of variation. It can be used to get a clearer picture of the relationships among the original variables. If the original variables have been selected well, so that they record information representing the important under-lying dimensions, then the components that emerge from analysis may correspond to these dimensions. For example, if instead we had recorded

Table 6.8 Principal components of scrambled egg

	PC1	PC2
Albumin	−0.367	0.929
Yellow	0.958	0.067
Palmitic acid	0.949	0.156
Vitamin D	0.790	0.163
Variance explained	64%	23%

vitamin C content, temperature and position in the cooking pan as original variables instead, the analysis of scrambled egg might not have distinguished yolk and white as successfully as it did.

Individual samples can be given a score on each of the newly derived principal components. Some statistical software packages can calculate such scores for you using a method similar to multiple regression. However, it is also possible to generate quick and dirty scores by hand. You first standardize scores on the original variables. Then sum the standard scores for the sample on each variable with a high loading on the component. For example, the PC1 score for the first sample would be the sum of its standard scores on the variables yellowness, palmitic acid and vitamin D content. You repeat this for each sample in turn. For example, the variables with high loadings on PC1 are yellowness, palmic acid and vitamin D content. Standard scores for the first sample are — 0.283 (yellow), −0.543 (palmic acid), −0.757 (vitamin D). Thus, we calculate a rough PC1 score for the first sample of −1.584, the sum of these standard scores. Component scores calculated in this way are not statistically pristine, but for practical purposes they will often do. Once you have created component scores, they can be used instead of the original variables in subsequent analyses. Using a small number of component variables which represent the principal dimensions of variation rather than a large number of observed variables can make analysis more manageable.

Usually it is best to base PCA on the matrix of correlations among the observed variables. The alternative is to use covariances. The advantage of using correlations is that this standardizes the observed variables so that superficial differences between scales of measurement do not distort the analysis. If covariances are used as the basis for analysis, component loadings are not literally correlations.

Factor analysis is very similar to PCA (Kline, 1994). Both approaches reduce a large set of observed variables to a small number of dimensions summarizing the relationships among the original variables. The difference between the two techniques lies in precisely what variance they attempt to account for. Principal components analysis accounts for all the variation in the original data. This includes shared variance lying in the overlap between variables, unique variance and error variance. Factor analysis accounts only for shared variance. You can confirm this by carrying out an analysis in which you have the same number of factors, or components, as original variables. Add up the amount of variance the components account for. In factor analysis, this will total less than 100%, but for PCA, it will come to 100%. Principal components analysis accounts for all the variance in the observed variables.

The result of either factor analysis or PCA can be subjected to a process termed rotation. Rotation involves realigning the components extracted in relation to the observed variables. The effect is to change the loadings of each observed variable on the components. This re-alignment can make it easier to see a coherent relationship between the observed variables and the components, and therefore make the components more interpretable. There are many kinds of rotation. The primary distinction is between orthogonal and oblique methods. The components directly extracted are always orthogonal. This means that there is no correlation between the components: they account for separate and non-overlapping parts of the variance. An orthogonal rotation maintains this. An oblique rotation allows rotated components to be correlated with one another. For many purposes, you will not mind if the components are correlated. However, if you plan to use component variables in subsequent analyses there may be some advantage in sticking to an orthogonal rotation.

6.6   SUMMARY

Exploratory techniques can be used to get a clearer picture of your data. It is often fruitful to apply such techniques to the residuals of an analysis since patterns there are patterns not already accounted for by your model. However, you have to bear in mind the problem of multiplicity and be cautious about drawing firm conclusions on the basis of an exploratory analysis. Setting up a further study to investigate any discoveries is appropriate.

A variety of techniques can be used to display multivariate data. This can be useful in helping to identify clusters or reduce the dimensionality of the data.

7 ANALYSIS OF VARIANCE IN COMPLEX DESIGNS

ANOVA is a flexible method of data analysis that can be applied in a general way to a range of different experimental designs. In some cases, there are particular considerations that arise. This chapter illustrates ways in which ANOVA can be applied in more complex designs.

7.1 HIGHER ORDER FACTORIAL DESIGNS

You can design an experiment with more than just two explanatory variables. For example, you might be interested in studying how long children take to complete a task. You think that three variables may influence this: age, sex and instructions given. All three can be included in the design for your study and analysed with a three-way ANOVA. In a three-way design, the ANOVA tests seven different effects. The effects tested would be the three main effects of the variables in the design, three two-way interactions corresponding to each pair of variables, and one three-way interaction. For this example, the model would be M7.1.

M7.1: time = age + sex + instructions + age * sex + age * instructions + sex * instructions + sex * instructions * age

The main effects are interpreted in the same way as main effects in a two-way or one-way ANOVA. For example, the main effect of *age* tests whether there is a difference on average between older and younger children.

Each of the two-way interactions is interpreted like the two-way interaction in a two-way ANOVA. It tests whether the effects of the predictor variables are independent. For example, if the two-way interaction of *age * sex* is significant this implies that the difference between older and younger children varies between boys and girls. That is, the effect of *age* depends on whether you are talking about boys or girls. Several different patterns of results can lead to a significant interaction, as we saw earlier. In this case, let's assume that for boys there is no difference between older and younger children but that older girls are faster than younger ones. This pattern is depicted in Fig. 7.1.

The three-way interaction is slightly more complex to understand. It tests whether any of the two-way interactions depends on the third variable. For example, it could be that when children are given video instructions, both boys and girls show significant differences between the 5 and 7 years age groups. However, when the instructions are presented through written or spoken language, only girls show improvement between the ages tested. Then the interaction of *age * sex* varies between the different sets of instructions, and so the three-way interaction is significant. When you find a significant higher order interaction, you need to take it into account when you interpret lower order effects. In this example, because of the three-way interaction, you have to qualify the two-way interaction. The three-way interaction gives a more finely differentiated analysis of the same data. It breaks the two-way interaction down into separate two-way tests for each level of the instruction type variable. If those two-way tests show the same pattern at each level, there is no interaction. If they show a different pattern at each level, then the two-way effect, which ignores differences in instruction type and will not have taken this into account, cannot be taken at face value. This is an important benefit of factorial designs. The higher order interactions open

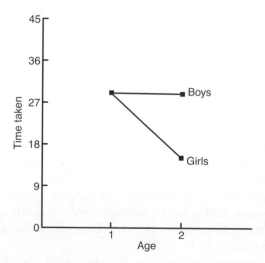

Figure 7.1 Two-way interaction between age and sex

up simpler effects and scrutinize their relationship with other variables.

Higher order designs are essentially the same as simpler designs, they just contain additional explanatory variables in the model. The main difference is the addition also of corresponding higher order interactions among these variables. These higher order interactions can be difficult to interpret. As with two-way interactions, it is important to look at cell means to try to understand the differences that gave rise to the interaction. You can add three, four, five or as many additional predictor variables as you like to the model. Each additional variable represents additional control and precision in your design. However, when you have more than four or five variables in the model, the higher order interactions become difficult to interpret. In addition, as the number of variables increases, the number of cells in the design increases. The three-way design we just discussed has 12 cells (2 ages × 2 sexes × 3 kinds of instructions). This requires 12 different groups of subjects. If you design the study to look also at, say, time of day of testing (morning versus afternoon) and socio-economic status of parents (four levels, A–D, reflecting income and education), then the design has 96 cells. A balanced study with this many cells will be costly to run. When the number of explanatory variables is high, it can be more appropriate to use multiple regression to analyse the data.

The experimental designs we have considered so far have been relatively straightforward between-subjects designs. The subjects in each condition are different people. In between-subjects designs there is a single estimate of error (MS_{error}) which is used in all F-ratios. However, in other designs, error is estimated slightly differently. We turn now to look at repeated-measures designs and other designs in which this is the case.

7.2   REPEATED MEASURES

In psychological experiments, the subjects are individuals — normally people. These individuals naturally vary in many ways brought about by their experience and their genetic endowment. In any particular experiment the vast majority of these differences are of no interest. The researcher is normally interested in systematic influences that affect the behaviour of people generally, rather than idiosyncracies that perturb particular individuals.

Nevertheless, these idiosyncratic differences are brought to the experimental situation by each subject and affect their responses. As we saw in Chapter 3, the general linear model assumes that the background noise these idiosyncracies create will be reflected in a normally distributed residual variance, with a mean of zero. In addition, the logic of the inferences made using tests like ANOVA or multiple regression requires that all differences between cases that might influence the outcome, other than those manipulated in the experiment, must be controlled.

For example, when you allocate children to groups in the study described earlier, if it happens that children in different groups have different levels of reading ability, the conclusions drawn will be undermined. If, say, girls allocated to the written instructions condition in the older age group have a superior reading ability to other girls, then this may be the explanation for a significant interaction between age and sex. Rather than the difference arising because of differences in the way boys versus girls respond to different forms of instruction, it could be merely an artefact of the greater reading skill advantage of older girls in one condition. Unless differences in reading ability are controlled, it will not be possible to untangle these rival explanations.

There are different ways in which you can control the effects of variables that might influence results. In a between-groups design, the allocation of subjects to groups is used to exercise this control. Subjects are assigned to groups randomly. This is vital to the logic of statistical inference. When subjects are assigned randomly to groups, there should in principle be no difference, on average, in the long run, between the groups on any extraneous variable. This allows you to conclude that any differences that emerge between the groups when you subject them to different conditions are due to the difference created by your manipulation of the conditions.

It is important to follow this procedure strictly. Even relatively innocent looking ways of assigning subjects to groups can introduce bias. For example, assigning children to groups on the basis of their seating position in class would introduce bias if their seating positions were determined by their teacher to reflect ability or behaviour, or if children choose their own seats and so sit near friends. Any procedure for assigning subjects to groups that is not random undermines the conclusions you draw from the study.

Assigning subjects randomly to groups in a between-groups design is one way of controlling sources of variance that may influence the results. There are other ways of achieving this. When a systematic source of error variance can be identified, it may be preferable to isolate this as an additional variable in the model. Alternatively, if each subject is tested repeatedly so that they experience all the conditions, then they will counterbalance themselves. The idiosyncracies of individual subjects will be balanced across the cells of the design.

We will use an example of an investigation into conceptual representation to illustrate the way designs can be selected to control the effects of a variable like subjects which you suspect may be systematically affecting scores. The question 'Is a horse an animal?' is a question about categorization — do objects which are horses belong to the category of animals? Such questions have been used to study subjects' representation of knowledge. A standard finding is that it is easier to answer the question when the candidate (horse) is a clear example of the category. When the candidate is a borderline example, 'Is a tomato a fruit?', subjects take longer to respond. Findings like this have led some psychologists to propose that knowledge about categories includes a representation of prototypes for categories. On this view, categorization judgements involve comparing the candidate with a prototype for the category. The closer the candidate is to the prototype, the faster the judgement can be made. Related to this is the finding that negative judgements are also harder to make when the candidate is borderline, 'Is a tomato a vegetable?', than when the decision is clear cut, 'Is a bison a vegetable?'.

Imagine the following hypothetical experiment extending these findings to judgements about football teams. One problem with the view as outlined is that the prototype is expected to be the average or typical example of the category. However, for some categories, this is not obviously correct. For example, although when subjects are asked to name examples of, say, vegetables, they do tend to name average ones first, there are other categories for which that does not seem intuitively likely. For example, if you were asked to give some examples of movie stars, are the names that come to mind first names like Humphrey Bogart and Robert Redford? Or are they names like Larry Hagman? It does seem intuitively that famous or ideal instances of the category are more prototypical if we operationalize prototypicality as order of mention. We could test this intuition more formally by setting up an experiment. Let's use the reaction time paradigm again. We will ask subjects categorization questions about soccer clubs. If this category is organized around an ideal, responses for successful clubs should be more rapid than responses for less successful ones. That is, we shall predict that the higher a team is in the league, the faster subjects will be able to answer the question 'Is this team a soccer team?'. So, for example, 'Is Manchester United a soccer team?' should be answered more quickly than 'Is Colchester United a soccer team?'. If this hypothesis is supported, then there will be some evidence that the reaction time for category judgements for soccer teams does depend on comparison to a prototype, but that the prototype is based on an ideal team rather than a typical team.

Let's initially consider a between-subjects design. Subjects are split into three groups. The first group is given only clubs from the Premier Division, the second group are asked only about Division Two clubs, and the third group is asked only about non-league clubs. The predictor variable is the division the clubs being asked about come from. In other words, variance in RT is to be explained in terms of the division the candidate is in and error variance.

There are, however, obvious problems with running an experiment like this as a between-subjects design. Not everyone is interested in soccer. Some people are very keen supporters and know a great deal; others think a corner kick is a peculiar assault most likely to occur in an octagonal room. There will be vast individual differences in knowledge about soccer among the subjects. The experimenter running a between-subjects design is relying on the random assignment of subjects to the three groups to iron these differences out. He hopes that random assignment will see that there is the same number of experts and novices in each group. However, for this to work either the individual differences have to be pretty small to begin with, or else there must be a large number of subjects in each group. In the case of soccer knowledge, the differences may be big and will almost certainly affect reaction times. Individual differences will inflate error variance. That is, because subjects in each group are very different, the scores in each group will vary a great deal. This means that the within group variance is high and therefore that error variance is high.

A second difficulty with using the between-groups design arises if individual differences have a systematic effect on the relationship between the dependent variable and the experimental variable. This is quite plausible in our example. It might be that subjects with no interest in football have no prototype for football teams, but instead use some other kind of representation, while fans do use prototypes. In this case, lumping the two kinds of subject together will mask the true patterns.

As the design stands, the only protection against the influence of individual differences is the random assignment of subjects to conditions. We need a better way to control for individual differences. The first approach to consider is the randomized blocks design.

7.2.1 Randomised blocks

You group subjects according to their level of interest in football. The design is exemplified in Table 7.1. You now have nine groups of subjects. The *interest* variable represents the likely prior knowledge of the subject. We have introduced what amounts to a second predictor variable in the design. Computation and analysis is exactly as if for two-way ANOVA. The model is M7.2.

Table 7.1 Randomized blocks design

	G1 (Premier Div.)	G2 (Division Two)	G3 (Non-league)
E1 (Enthusiastic)			
E2 (Med. interest)			
E3 (No interest)			

M7.2: data = division + interest + division * interest + error

You have moved one aspect of individual difference, soccer interest, out of error and into the model. This should reduce the size of the error term and thus give a more sensitive test of the hypothesis we are really interested in: does team quality affect categorization judgement? We now also have an interaction term which can tell us whether the effect of team quality depends on prior knowledge. This lets us deal with the second difficulty mentioned above: do novices and experts use the same kind of representation?

You could assign subjects to groups by asking them a single question, 'How interested are you in soccer?', and using the answer to assign them to a group. This is not completely fruity. If you do it this way, in the write up you say something like 'subjects were assigned to groups on the blocking variable using a measure of enthusiasm based on self-report . . .'. Alternatively, you might use a questionnaire, a test, the judgement of the subject's class teacher or some other more objective device to assign subjects to groups.

A randomized blocks design allows you to control for a portion of variance due to individual differences by making the relevant individuality an explicit part of the model. The extent to which it can effectively improve the power of your test of the primary hypothesis depends on several considerations.

First, of course, it depends on how much the facet of individual difference you pick on actually does affect the dependent variable. For example, you could divide subjects into subgroups using hair colour as a blocking variable. But hair colour is unlikely to affect reaction times in the example just discussed.

Second, it depends, of course, on how valid and reliable the measure is that you use to assess the blocking variable. If the variable is not measured well, blocking will not be effective.

Third, it is affected by how many groups you divide subjects into on the blocking variable. If you use too few groups, you will not really be tackling the problem. The extreme case is to use just one group, i.e. do not block subjects at all. Obviously, if you use too few groups you will not differentiate sufficiently among subjects. On the other hand, there is a trade-off here. Use too many groups and you will get hit by the law of diminshing returns.

Increasingly fine distinctions among subjects will produce increasingly small reductions in error variance. The cost of making extra distinctions (i.e. having more levels on the blocking variable) is twofold. First, it is more trouble to have more groups. Second, each extra group costs you one degree of freedom for the error term. Blocking pays only when the gain in reducing error variance can offset the cost of losing degrees of freedom.

Reducing error variance should improve your *F*-ratio. The bigger the *F*-ratio is, the better the chance of statistical significance. At the same time, for any given value of *F*, the more degrees of freedom there are, the better the chance of statistical significance.

7.2.2 Repeated measures

In a randomized blocks design, we lift one facet of individual difference out of error variance and put it explicitly into the model. Repeated measures designs remove all differences among subjects from the error term, and place a new explanatory variable, subjects, into the model. In a pure repeated measures design, each subject participates in all the conditions of the experiment. It is as if we introduced a blocking variable *subjects* into the design with the same number of levels as there are subjects. That is, each subject constitutes an individual subgroup. For example, our semantic memory and soccer study would have the layout indicated in Table 7.2 (assuming three subjects; you would usually have more!).

Another example: an experimenter might be interested in measuring reading time for three kinds of text: normal text, syntactic text and random text. Syntactic text obeys the rules of grammar, but makes no sense semantically; random text is a sequence of words that does not even follow rules of grammar. The experimenter has 12 subjects and tests each subject in each of the three conditions. Data is gathered in the form indicated in Table 7.3. Thus, each subject contributes a single score to

Table 7.2 Within-subjects design

	G1 (Premier Div.)	G2 (Division Two)	G3 (Non-league)
Subject one			
Subject two			
Subject three			

Table 7.3 Illustrative language scores

Subject	Condition	Score
1	Normal	3.23
1	Syntactic	4.57
1	Random	4.94
2	Normal	2.92
2	Syntactic	3.51
2	Random	4.25
⋮	⋮	⋮

each condition. This is a within-subjects or repeated measures design. The advantages are twofold. First, we are controlling for individual differences. In a between-subjects design (one-way) the model looks like M7.3.

M7.3: data = textype + error

Here, *error* includes both variance due to random error and variance due to differences between subjects. In a repeated measures design, subject effects are treated as a separate variable, as shown in M7.4.

M7.4: data = textype + subjects + error

By taking variance due to subjects out of the error term, we gain a more powerful test of the effect we are interested in. When subject variance comes out of error, the size of the error is reduced. Because the error is used as the denominator in the *F*-test, the smaller the error is, the higher the *F*-ratio will be. This reduction in error, then, makes our *F*-test more powerful. The second advantage lies in reducing the number of subjects needed. By recycling subjects and using them over again in a number of conditions we conserve a scarce resource. A repeated measures design uses as its error term the interaction of the effect of interest with subjects. Thus M7.4 can be expressed more precisely as M7.5.

M7.5: data = textype + subjects + subjects * textype

Each subject supplies only one score for each condition. There is therefore no within-subjects variance and so we cannot use within-subjects variance as the error term. The best estimate we can get of residual error is the *subjects * textype* interaction. This interaction term provides an exact estimate of error for the main effect of *textype*. In other words, the *F*-ratio formed by dividing MS_{textype} by MS_{T*S} gives an exact test of the main effect of this variable. However, you cannot use MS_{T*S} to make an exact test of the significance of the effect of subjects because it would underestimate the significance. This is not generally a problem because the effect of subjects is rarely of direct interest, and is normally highly significant anyway. An imaginary ANOVA table for an experiment with a design like this is shown in Table 7.4.

In general, to test any effect in a repeated measures design, use as the error term the interaction of that effect with subjects.

Table 7.4 Layout of ANOVA table for within-subjects designs

Source	SS	df	MS	F	p
Textype	1.71	2	0.856	4.21	> 0.10
$S \times T$	0.81	4	0.204		

7.2.3 Assumptions of repeated measures designs

Instead of assuming homogeneity of variance across cells as a between-subjects design does, repeated measures ANOVA assumes the homogeneity of variance of difference scores across cells. This assumption is called sphericity. You could directly test it by setting up a table like Table 7.5. This table has one row for each subject.

The assumption is met if the variances of the last three columns are broadly similar. You could test this by doing side by side box and whisker plots of these difference columns. If this assumption is violated, there is an increased possibility that chance differences will be declared statistically significant. For psychological data, this assumption is almost never met. This means that for repeated measures designs the *p*-values printed by ANOVA are not precisely correct.

There are different views on how best to deal with this problem. There are two choices, and most statistical software packages make these choices available. The first option is to adjust the *p*-value slightly to take into account the effect of failing to meet the assumption. This can be done using a correction formula which reduces the degrees of freedom in proportion to the extent to which the assumption is violated. The greater the violation, the more the degrees of freedom are reduced. When the degrees of freedom are reduced, the critical value for the *F*-ratio is raised and so statistical significance is tested against a slightly more severe criterion. The observed *F*-ratio needs to be higher to be considered significant. Both the Greenhouse–Geisser correction and the Huynh–Feldt adjustment achieve this by calculating a value called epsilon ϵ which estimates the extent to which the assumption is violated. This value ϵ is then used to scale back the degrees of freedom used to check whether the *F*-ratio is significant. These approaches vary in the way ϵ is

Table 7.5 Testing the sphericity assumption

Subject	N	S	R	R–S	S–N	R–N
1	3.23	4.57	4.94	4.94–4.57	4.57–3.23	4.94–3.23
2	2.92	3.51	4.25	4.25–3.51	3.51–2.92	4.25–2.92
⋮	⋮	⋮	⋮	⋮	⋮	⋮

That is:

Subject	N	S	R	R–S	S–N	R–N
1	3.23	4.57	4.94	0.37	1.34	1.71
2	2.92	3.51	4.25	0.74	0.59	1.33
⋮	⋮	⋮	⋮	⋮	⋮	⋮

calculated. In general, they will produce very similar inferences about significance.

The second option is to use a multivariate ANOVA to test significance. The multivariate test examines a slightly different hypothesis from the standard test, and it may not always be appropriate. Multivariate ANOVA tests whether the pattern of response across trials is the same for the groups being compared. However, the multivariate test does not make the sphericity assumption, and so its conclusions hold good even when there is no sphericity. Many statistics programs will print out multivariate tests alongside the classic repeated measures ANOVA. If the inferences suggested by these statistics are consistent with those drawn by applying a correction to the classic repeated measures ANOVA, then all is well. If the ordinary repeated measures statistics are significant but the multivariate ones are not, unfortunately sphericity got you.

It is worth noting that when a within subjects variable has only two levels, the sphericity assumption does not bite. This is because with only two levels there is only one covariance.

7.2.4 Repeated measures on two variables

A fairly common design uses two repeated measures variables. For example, you might look at textype and text difficulty together. Text difficulty might be represented by two levels, hard and easy. Each subject now sees six passages, as indicated in Table 7.6.

The model statement for this design is shown in M7.6.

M7.6: data = textype | difficulty | textype * difficulty + subjects +
   S * T + S * D + S * T * D

Both predictors (*textype* and *difficulty*) are repeated measures variables, because the same subjects repeat at each level of the variable. Both *textype* and *difficulty* are also fixed in the sense discussed in Section 7.4. Table 7.7 is an imaginary ANOVA table for data of this kind. Each effect of interest is tested using its interaction with *subjects* as the denominator of the *F*-ratio.

Table 7.6 Illustrative language scores for two within-subjects variable designs

Subject	Textype	Difficulty	Score
1	Normal	Hard	3.23
1	Syntactic	Hard	4.57
1	Random	Hard	4.94
1	Normal	Easy	2.92
1	Syntactic	Easy	3.51
1	Random	Easy	4.25
⋮	⋮	⋮	⋮

Table 7.7   Layout of ANOVA table for two within-subjects variables designs

Source	SS	df	MS	F	p
Textype (T)	8.56	2	4.28	14.87	< 0.01
S × T	3.46	12	0.29		
Difficulty (D)	0.01	1	0.01	0.001	> 0.9
S × D	16.63	6	2.77		
T × D	0.61	2	0.30	0.27	> 0.7
S × T × D	13.79	12	1.15		

7.3   MIXED DESIGNS

The mixed design is possibly the most common design encountered in psychology. In this design, some explanatory variables are between-groups, other variables are repeated measures. For example, you might have textype as a repeated measures variable, and sex as a between-subjects variable. The model for this design is given in M7.7 and the layout of the design is exemplified in Table 7.8.

M7.7: data = textype + sex + textype * sex + subject/sex + subject * textype/sex

The last two terms are 'subjects within sex' and 'subjects by textype interaction within sex'. The *subjects* effects are calculated separately for each level of the between-subjects variable. This is necessary, of course, because the subjects are different people at each level of the between-subjects variable. These sums of squares for each level are simply added together to give the total effects 'subjects within sex' and 'subjects by textype interaction within sex' for the whole variable. 'Subjects within sex' is the error term for the between-subjects variable itself. 'Subjects by textype interaction within sex' is the error term for the within-subjects

Table 7.8   Illustrative language scores for mixed design

Subject	Textype	Gender	Score
1	Normal	Female	3.23
1	Syntactic	Female	4.57
1	Random	Female	4.94
2	Normal	Male	2.92
2	Syntactic	Male	3.51
2	Random	Male	4.25
⋮	⋮	⋮	⋮

Table 7.9 Layout of ANOVA table for mixed design

Source	SS	df	MS	F	p
Between subjects					
Gender (G)	0.64	1	0.64	1.18	> 0.25
S/G	3.24	6	0.54		
Within subjects					
Textype	8.61	2	4.31	5.44	< 0.05
G × T	0.38	2	0.19	0.24	> 0.25
S × T/G	9.50	12	0.79		

variable (*textype*) and the interaction it has with *sex*. The ANOVA table is laid out as shown in Table 7.9 with, once again, fictitious numbers.

7.4   FIXED AND RANDOM VARIABLES

The one-way repeated measures ANOVA is conceptually similar to a two-way ANOVA with subjects as the second explanatory variable. However, the levels of the subjects variable are slightly different from the levels of most variables we've looked at until now. Most variables we have looked at have a small number of levels which are in a sense fixed by the logic of the experiment. For example, if you were running the experiment again, you would almost certainly use the same levels of textype (normal, syntactic, random). These levels completely summarize the variable you are interested in. They represent the population of texts the way an ambassador represents a nation state. The ambassador represents her state by stipulation. It is just part of the definition of being an ambassador that you stand for your home country. The views of an ambassador are taken to be the views of her state. That is what ambassadors do. Subjects, on the other hand, speak for themselves. A subject is a loose cannon. Subjects represent a population the same way participants in an opinion poll do. Each subject represents their own view. By taking a random sample, and by sampling enough people, the pollster hopes to arrive at a representative cross-section of views. In this way, the opinion poll sample represents the population. For example, if you want to know what France thinks of monetary union, you can poll a sample of people, or ask the ambassador. If you want to ask the same question again (perhaps in 12 months' time) then, again, you can either take a sample or ask the ambassador. The crucial difference is that this time your poll sample will consist of different people. You will get a fresh sample. But the ambassador is an institution and does not change, even if the identity of the person occupying the office changes, short of a revolution at home.

This distinction has statistical consequences. If your explanatory variable has fixed effects, then its levels have an ambassadorial obligation, no choice but to represent the variable, and the values of these effects should sum to zero. For example, if the variable is age, you put subjects into age groups representing the range of ages of interest. Let's say we are interested in the relationship between age and wine appreciation. The age groups might be 18–24, 25–34, 35–50, 50+ . These groups have no choice but to represent the range of ages of interest, and so age is a fixed variable. The dependent variable will be some measure of wine appreciation. Assume scores range from 0–20. Our statistical analysis partitions the variance in scores according to the usual model for a one-way ANOVA:

M7.8: data = age + error

We interpret the effect of *age* as a perturbation on the grand mean that varies with age. For example, the effect at 18–24 might be −3. The effect at 25–34 might be + 4. And so on. The vital thing is that we expect these effects to sum to zero. After all, the grand mean is the grand mean. In other words, the different effects of a fixed variable are expected to balance out. With a random variable, such as *subjects*, where the levels are set at random and where levels are loose cannons, we can in general have no such expectation. The effects of the levels of a random variable are not expected to sum to zero.

This difference between fixed and random variables has consequences in the mathematical background to ANOVA. You do not need to worry about this background in itself. However, you do need to be aware of the distinction between fixed and random variables and to be aware that it has consequences for the availability and correct choice of error terms to test hypotheses. For example, if you have one random variable, usually subjects, you can only make a negatively biased F-test of it, i.e. an underestimate of its effect. If you have two random variables there may be no exact test even of the other fixed effects in the design.

The random variable you are most likely to encounter is the subjects variable in repeated measures and mixed designs. However, you may wish to treat an items variable as a random variable. For example, if you test subjects on a list of words, each word you select for the list is one of all the possible words you could have used. For example, if we ask people about tomatoes and cabbages, these are nouns sampled from the set of all nouns denoting vegetables. If you want to generalize the conclusions of your experiment to all nouns, then you should treat noun as a random variable in your model. Because of the difficulty of calculating appropriate values when there are two random variables, many experimenters will run two separate analyses. One analysis is done by subjects, and contains subjects but not items as a variable. The other is done by items. You then check that effects are significant in both analyses.

7.5 LATIN SQUARES

The latin square is a way of identifying a systematic subset of possible treatment combinations. Latin squares are used to set up the design of an experiment, but when they are used to do this they should also be taken into account in the statistical analysis. Examples of latin squares for different sizes of design are given in advanced texts such as Myers and Well (1991). There are two common reasons for using latin squares. The first is to control order effects, the second is to select a practicable subset of conditions that can be run in a study where to run all permutations of explanatory variables would be too costly.

When the same subject participates in more than one trial, the possibility arises that the response on the second trial was influenced by participation in the first trial. Influences like this are called carry-over effects. The second response could improve because of learning, or it could become worse because of fatigue. If every subject undertook the conditions in the same order there would be no way to disentangle the effect of order from the effect of the difference between the conditions. The two would be confounded.

If the number of conditions is small, then control can be achieved by counterbalancing the order in which conditions are presented. For example, if there are two conditions, half the subjects can get condition A first, the remainder get condition B followed by A. If you counterbalance the design of your study to control for order effects, then it is best to include order as a term in the statistical model. This lets you test whether there were order effects in your study.

The number of conditions can be prohibitively large, however. For example, if each subject is tested on each word in a list of 30, then trying to counterbalance the order of presentation is impractical. In this situation, you can just randomize the order of presentation of words for each subject. Alternatively, you can generate a small number of lists, say three or four, each containing the words in a different random order. Each subject is then randomly assigned to one of the lists. In this case, list can be included as a term in your model, allowing you to test whether there was an order effect.

When you include order in your model, if the main effect of order and any interactions with other effects are not significant, then it is sensible to drop it from the model. You then recalculate the ANOVA including only the remaining terms. In your report you would write something like: 'neither the effect of order nor its interaction with other variables was significant and so in the analyses reported data are pooled across orders.'

In some circumstances, these devices for controlling order may not suffice. For example, you may wish to present the lists of words to each subject several times, once under each of a number of conditions. For instance, you might want to present them to subjects after varying periods of starvation. Each subject is tested, say, one hour, two hours, four hours and eight hours after their last meal. Obviously, you cannot present each subject with the same list of words four times. You could prepare a different list for each time period, but if every subject got the same list as the others, the list would be confounded with time delay. This would mean you could not tell whether effects of time delay were actually just due to differences between the lists. A latin square can be used to distribute the lists systematically across subjects and time delays. For example, one subject would have list A at the first time period, list B at the second, list C at the third, list D at the fourth. Meanwhile, another subject would have list D at the first, list C at the second, list B at the third and list A at the fourth. The latin square design ensures that each list appears equally often at each time delay, and that each subject receives each of the lists exactly once.

In the previous example, the latin square enabled us to avoid presenting every logical combination of list and time delay to every subject. It would not have been practical to give every subject all four lists at each time delay. Indeed, that would have vitiated the purpose of having four different lists. Sometimes it is useful to use a latin square to reduce the number of cells in a design just because it saves time testing. For example, you might want to investigate the efficacy of different teaching methods (say whole class versus group versus a mixture of both) in different kinds of school (say comprehensive school, selective state school or private school) on different days of the week. A $3 \times 3 \times 5$ design has 45 cells. Judicious use of a latin square may allow you to reduce the amount of testing needed to assess your hypothesis. However, because not all possible combinations of variables are tested, not all of the terms available in a factorial ANOVA can be tested. In particular, you need to bear in mind that interaction terms cannot be tested properly, and to the extent that there are interactions among the variables, the power of the F-tests of the factors of primary interest is reduced. Using this strategy successfully requires you to be clear about just what hypothesis you want to test but then can give you benefit of requiring only as much empirical work as is necessary to test that hypothesis.

7.6　SUMMARY

Models can be constructed which take into account the influence of many variables, and the interactions of one predictor with another. Variables may be included in the design to allow potential sources of error that randomization may not control. By extracting sources of variance from error and accounting for them explicitly in the model, more powerful tests of hypotheses can sometimes be made.

8 COMPARISONS AND CONTRASTS

When you start to analyse a set of data, you begin with EDA and then move on to test your hypotheses with inferential statistics. Often, especially in the case of a designed experiment, you will choose the ANOVA as the initial statistic to use. This chapter discusses other inferential statistics that can be used alongside ANOVA to test questions that the overall ANOVA statistic may not have settled.

8.1 THE GLOBAL NATURE OF ANOVA TESTS

When you run an ANOVA, you get tests of the significance of the main effects of the predictor variables, and of the interactions between the predictors. However, each of these tests is global in the sense that it tests an overall comparison across all levels of the particular factor, or interaction.

For example, you might test three groups of subjects for their ability on a learning task. The three groups have different levels of problem: group A are easy, group B medium difficulty and group C are hard. For each subject, you record a score representing the number of errors on a subsequent test. You use ANOVA to test the significance of the differences between the groups. This would be a one-way ANOVA. The single variable would be difficulty (with 3 levels, A–C), and of course there would be no interaction term. Analysis of variance here will give you a single test of the main effect of difficulty. This is sometimes called an omnibus test. Let's say that this is statistically significant, what you can infer is that overall, across the three groups A–C, the means are further apart than one would expect them to be if the groups were performing identically. In other words, the means of the groups are significantly different.

The crucial thing is to realize what the ANOVA cannot tell you. It cannot tell you whether each of the group means is significantly different from all the others, or whether for instance two of the means are actually fairly similar while only the third differs markedly. In other words, ANOVA only gives you an overall test of the differences between the means, and it will not tell you which particular means differ. Sometimes the overall tests are enough, but often you need more specific information.

8.2   GRAPHS

Sometimes people who are relatively good at maths have a tendency to disparage graphs and histograms, because they seem so easy to construct and so simple from the mathematical point of view. But the goal is to make the facts easy to perceive, and a graph can be the ideal tool. By laying out the data in a form that the eye can absorb immediately, you can pick out the patterns in the data that you need.

When you do an ANOVA and find that the main effect is too global for your needs, when you find that a main effect or interaction is glossing over the specific differences you want to test, the first thing to do is draw a graph plotting the means for the subgroups representing each level of the factor in question. For example, in our example you should draw a graph showing the average score for each of the groups A–C. From such a graph, you will be able to see what the relationships are among the means — are they all different, or are two fairly similar, for example? If all three differ from one another, a graph of the means could look like Fig. 8.1. The second pattern mentioned might look like Fig. 8.2, with groups B and C having relatively small differences between them.

Having seen the pattern in a graph, you may now have enough information to test your hypothesis. The graph itself may settle the question you were interested in. For example, if your hypothesis was that group B would make more errors than C, then either of the graphs just presented can refute your hypothesis. Although the main effect of difficulty was significant, the difference between B and C was simply in the wrong direction to support your hypothesis. There is therefore no need specifically to compare groups B and C alone with an inferential statistic. However, you may have predicted the opposite: the subjects with a harder task in C would score more errors than B. The graph shows the difference is in the right direction, but does not tell you if it is significant. In this case you will need to check the indication given by the graphs using an inferential statistic.

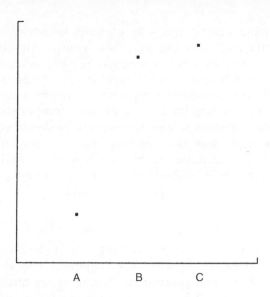

Figure 8.1 Means for three groups

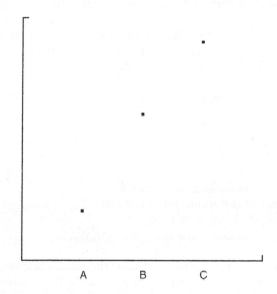

Figure 8.2 Means for three groups

8.3 PLANNED COMPARISONS

Let's assume that when you designed the experiment, you were specifically interested in the differences between medium and hard groups
(groups B and C). You thought that subjects in the hard problem group

would make more errors, and you planned in advance to test the significance of the difference between these groups. Although the main effect was significant, that is not enough. You are interested to know specifically whether B and C differ significantly. Because you always planned to make this particular comparison (between B and C), you are entitled to use a procedure for making planned comparisons.

A very general approach to comparisons can be described. It involves constructing an expression that identifies the comparision to be made among terms. In this example, there are three means, and we want to compare the second (B) with the third (C), disregarding the first (A). For this example, an appropriate expression would be:

contrast $= 0 + 1 - 1$

For each term there is a number indicating how it should participate in the comparison. These numbers are called contrast coefficients. There are two things to notice about contrast coefficients. They must always add up to a total of zero (thus $0 + 1 + (-1) = 0$). Second, the coefficients used for levels that are being compared should normally have the same magnitude, but they should have opposite signs (thus $1, -1$ for B and C respectively).

Many statistics programs allow you to enter a contrast in this form, and will calculate the effect for you. However, it is easy to calculate a contrast by hand. The formula is as follows:

$$F\,(1, df_{error}) = \frac{\psi / \Sigma\,(w_i / n_i)}{error}$$

where:
$\psi = \Sigma\,w_i / M_i$
w_i is the contrast coefficient for each cell
n_i is the number of observations in the cell
M_i is the observed mean of the cell
error is the mean square error from the ANOVA

ANOVA partitions the variance in your data into components that can be attributed to different sources of variation. In this example, it draws out variance that can be accounted for by differences between the three groups. This component is the between-groups variance. The other component is error variance. Thus, ANOVA divides the variance into two main parts. The contrast, in turn, draws out a component of the between-groups variance. This breaks the between-group variance into smaller parts. The contrast examines a specific aspect of the between-groups differences.

You can think of the main effect in this ANOVA as a set of hypotheses. It tests whether any of the following three hypotheses can be rejected:

(a) A = B; (b) A = C; (c) B = C. If it is significant, you know that at least one of them can be rejected, but not which one. The contrast identifies a specific comparison and selects it for testing.

In fact, there are many other comparisons that can be of interest. These comparisons correspond to specific hypotheses about the results. This technique can be extended to these other kinds of comparison. For example, you might believe that group A would be significantly different from groups B and C taken together. Thus, you would be comparing one group against two others considered as if they were a single group. This kind of comparison can be made by choosing contrast coefficients that reflect the groups being compared. To compare A against B and C you can use the contrast $2 - 1 - 1$. Alternatively, you might predict a linear trend across the three conditions. If you expect that A < B < C you could predict that the means will gradually increase across the three conditions. A contrast for this prediction would be $-1\ 0\ 1$.

8.4 *t*-TESTS FOR PLANNED COMPARISONS

An alternative approach to planned comparisons involves a simple extension to the ordinary *t*-test. The formula is given below. The only difference between this and an ordinary *t*-test lies in the way we estimate the error variance. For an ordinary *t*-test, we would base the error on the two groups being compared. Here we use the error mean square from the ANOVA. This is used because it gives a better estimate of the error variance, being based on a larger sample, as long as the homogeneity of variance assumption is satisfied, as discussed in Chapter 3.

The first of the two formulae here is used if the groups whose means are being compared have equal numbers of subjects. The second is used where the groups have different numbers of subjects. The degrees of freedom to use are the degrees of freedom of the error term in the main ANOVA.

$$t = \frac{M_1 - M_2}{\sqrt{\frac{2\,\text{error}}{n}}} \qquad t = \frac{M_1 - M_2}{\sqrt{\text{error}\left(\frac{1}{n_1} + \frac{1}{n_2}\right)}}$$

where: M_1 is the mean of the first group
M_2 is the mean of the second group
error is the error mean square from the ANOVA
n is the number of subjects in each group

Planned comparisons are legitimate where (a) the hypotheses you test with them flow meaningfully from the design of the experiment; and (b) you do only a small number of comparisons. If you do a large number of comparisons, or if you choose comparisons to test on the basis of the results of the experiment rather than its design, then the significance tests may be misleading. When a large number of comparisons is done, the problem of multiplicity discussed in Chapter 6 emerges. Because many comparisons are done, the chance increases of encountering one of those rare situations where an extreme difference occurs between samples from populations that do not in fact differ. In this situation, it may be appropriate to set a stricter criterion for statistical significance. The following section describes statistical tests that use different approaches to achieve this.

8.5   *POST HOC* COMPARISONS

Often researchers decide to make specific comparisons only because the difference between some pair of conditions turns out to be large. You look at the data, see a large difference and you want to be able to report this when you write up the study. You also want to know whether it should be given weight when you interpret the results and draw conclusions. When you select comparisons because you are seduced by temptations in the data, you need a conscience. The crucial thing to understand is that you are effectively trawling the entire set of possible comparisons. *Post hoc* comparisons consequently raise problems concerning the rate at which you make type I errors. As you know, the .05 significance level reflects differences so unusual you would only expect them five times in 100 if chance alone were at work. When you are making only one test you can be reasonably confident with this significance level. If, however, you make 20 comparisons then you would expect one of the 20 to have a difference this great by chance alone. A type I error occurs when you reject the hypothesis although it is true. Procedures for *post hoc* comparisons are all based on the idea that you need a way of taking into account this effect on the type I error rate. You need to be sure that you do not take advantage of the extra information you have after the experiment has been run.

We examine here four procedures for carrying out multiple comparisons. These procedures can be used either when you are carrying out many planned comparisons or when your comparisons have been selected *post hoc*. Like all multiple comparison procedures, they operate by setting a more stringent criterion for significance. They differ in the way that they do this and some make more stringent adjustments than others. They share the feature that the adjustment made takes into account the number of comparisons made. The more comparisons made, the tougher the criterion set by any of these procedures. For multiple planned comparisons, the number of comparisons is the number actually made. For *post hoc* comparisons, the number of comparisons made is the total number of comparisons you could make even if you have pulled out only one to test. Although four tests are listed, you are unlikely to use them all in any particular study. A short section below indicates how you can select which test is most appropriate.

1. The Bonferroni approach (also known as the Dunn procedure)
2. Tukey's Honestly Significant Difference
3. Newman–Keuls procedure
4. Scheffé's test

8.5.1 The Bonferroni approach

The Bonferroni approach is the most direct of the approaches considered here. In order to ensure that the chance of a type I error stays at your chosen α-level (.05, for example), you apply a stricter significance level. In other words, say you want to make five comparisons, and you want the real α-level to be .05 for all those comparisons. The Bonferroni approach says make all five comparisons; any which exceed the (stricter) .01 significance level you can have at the (desired) .05 level. You make the comparison using the usual test (typically an ordinary *t*-test). Then, instead of comparing with the critical value for .05, you have to compare with .01. Even if you exceed the critical value for .01, you are still allowed to claim only the .05 level.

This approach, then, makes a distinction between the actual significance level and the superficial significance level. The actual significance level is the probability in the real world that you would find such a large difference if there was no true difference. This actual significance level is, of course, the only one that matters. On the other hand, there is the superficial significance level. This is the significance level that you get if you look up your obtained value (of *t*, say) in the tables at the back of your book, or if you use the *p* value printed out by your statistics software. The superficial level is the likelihood of obtaining the observed difference by chance if no account is taken of the fact that this is one of many comparisions being done. If you make just one planned comparison, the superficial significance level and the actual significance level coincide. When you make many comparisons, they diverge because of the problem of multiplicity. The more *post hoc* comparisons you make on a given set of data, the more deceptive the superficial significance level is. All of the *post hoc* tests discussed here take account of this. They do it in different ways, and some are tougher than others. The Bonferroni approach simply says, if you want an actual significance level of .05, and you want to make *n* comparisons, then you had better check your obtained values using the superficial significance level of .05/n. When you look up the tables, if you want .05, look up

.05/n. For example, if n is 2 (you are making two comparisons) to be absolutely sure any differences are significant at .05, look up the tables for .025 (.05/2). If the differences (superficially) exceed .025, then you can legitimately claim that they actually exceed .05. This method gives you an actual significance level of .05.

The obvious difficulty you will encounter with this approach is that the tables of critical values of t which many textbooks reproduce in an appendix do not provide all the significance levels you might need. However, they do provide a reasonable selection (.1, .05, .025, .01, .005 and .0005 in some books), and it is not unreasonable to round your superficial significance level to the nearest significance level available. So, if you want three comparisons at the .05 level (superficial level needs to be .05/3 = .0166) you could use the .01 tables.

If you always round down, then you will not be liberalizing the type I error rate, but you may miss some differences which ought to be declared significant. If you are bothered by this dilemma, compare the obtained value with the critical values for the tables on both sides (in our example with .0166 as the superficial error rate, these neighbours would be .01 and .025). If both superficial rates give the same outcome, your worries are over.

To calculate a Bonferroni t-test, then, calculate an ordinary t-test, but for an α-level α, look up the tables for α/n, where n is the number of comparisons you want to make. The Bonferroni approach is extremely useful because it is not limited to the t-test. The same technique can be used effectively with almost any statistic. You could use this approach for correlations, F-tests or even non-parametric tests. Whenever you want to control the type I error rate in the face of a multiplicity of tests, the Bonferroni approach can help. You should also use this approach if you are making planned comparisons but the number of comparisons is large.

8.5.2 Studentized statistics

The Bonferroni approach can be used with any statistic. However, a number of tests have been developed which employ a statistic known as the studentized range. The studentized range is one of a small set of 'studentized' statistics you might come across. Another is the student-ized residual. Studentized statistics are statistics whose values have been transformed, rather in the way that raw scores are transformed into z-scores. When raw scores are transformed to z-scores, they are standardized against a normal distribution. When a statistic is studentized, it is standardized onto a t-distribution. (The statistician who invented the t-test always called himself Student in published work. His employer was the brewer Guinness.) In the same way that we can immediately look up the significance of a standard score, studentized statistics can be compared directly with significance tables.

8.5.3 Tukey's Honestly Significant Difference

This is one of a number of *post hoc* tests based on the studentized range, which make use of the reference value Q. These tests are suitable only for making comparisons between individual group means, but can be used to make many such comparisons. Tukey's Honestly Significant Difference (HSD) is the easiest to calculate. However, it is less powerful than other tests based on Q because it sets a stringent test for significance. This means that differences have to be larger for Tukey's HSD to find them significant.

In general, Tukey's test involves comparing values of Q obtained from your data with critical values of Q. To be statistically significant, the obtained value must exceed the corresponding critical value. There are different critical values for different numbers of degrees of freedom and different numbers of groups being compared. The formula for obtained values of Q is:

$$Q = \frac{M_1 - M_2}{\sqrt{\frac{error}{n}}}$$

Here, error is the error term used in the main ANOVA (i.e. the within-groups sum of squares in a one way design). Also, n is the number of subjects in each group. Calculating Q is very similar to calculating t. With Q, M_2 is always the smaller of the two being compared. You calculate a separate obtained value of Q for each comparison that you want to make. You then compare each of these obtained values with the critical value for Q.

With Tukey's test, you use a single critical value to check all your obtained values. The degrees of freedom for this critical value are the degrees of freedom of the error term you are using. You can get the degrees of freedom for this error term from the main ANOVA table. You also need to know the number of groups being compared (k). Once you have the df and k, you can look up the critical value. Any obtained values that exceed this critical value are statistically significant.

The significance of Q can be determined using tables found in many textbooks. You need two numbers to identify the critical value of Q in the table. This critical value is the value your obtained Q must exceed if the difference is significant. You need the degrees of freedom (df) and the number of means in the set your comparisons are drawn from (k). The appropriate value for df is the degrees of freedom associated with the error term of the F-ratio used to calculate F. In general, this is the denominator of the *F*-ratio used to test the main effect (e.g. difficulty) in the initial ANOVA. The value of *k* in our case would be 3, since difficulty has three levels. If the obtained value exceeds the critical value, then the obtained value is statistically significant.

8.5.4 The Newman–Keuls method

The Newman–Keuls method is another test based on the studentized range which makes use of *Q* as a reference value. It is slightly more lenient than Tukey's HSD. That is, it will declare smaller differences significant. On the other hand, it is more tedious to work out. Here is an example. Three groups of students are asked to tie their shoelaces. Group A is left-handed, Group B is right-handed and group C tie the laces on a dummy. The dependent variable is the time taken to complete the task. The means for the three groups are 4, 6 and 18 seconds respectively. The overall *F*-test is significant (the MS_{error} is 26.38, df = 12).

You calculate *Q* separately for each possible pair of means, and compare these obtained *Q*s with criterion values of *Q* taken from tables. The obtained value of Q is:

$$Q = \frac{M_1 - M_2}{\sqrt{\frac{error}{n}}}$$

Here, error is the denominator of the *F*-ratio used to test the main effect (e.g. group) in the initial ANOVA, and *n* is the number of subjects in each group. In other words, this is exactly the same formula used to calculate obtained values for *Q* in Tukey's test. For example, *Q* for the comparison of groups A and C would be:

$$Q_{A,C} = \frac{18 - 4}{\sqrt{\frac{26.38}{5}}} = 6.095$$

You could calculate obtained values of *Q* for the two other contrasts as an exercise.

So far, the process of calculation is identical to that used for Tukey's HSD. The difference lies in the process of comparing the obtained values with critical values. The criterion values of *Q* are found in tables using df = 'df associated with error', and with *k* set according to the number of steps apart the means being compared are in a rank ordering of all the means being considered. In other words, all the means are ordered from lowest to highest. When adjacent means are being compared, k = 2.

When they are one place apart in the ordering, k = 3. When they are two places apart in the ordering, k = 4. And so on. Thus different comparisons not only have different obtained values of Q, they may also have different critical values for Q. Obtained and critical values are then compared to see which obtained values exceed their critical value and can therefore be declared significant.

In our example, df = 12, k = 2 (for A–B, B–C), k = 3 (for A–C). If we choose an α-level of .05, we get the following critical values for Q: 3.08 (k = 2); 3.77 (k = 3). As an exercise, check tables of the Studentized Range Statistic (Q) to make sure these values are correct.

There is, however, another difference between the Newman–Keuls procedure and Tukey's HSD. The comparisons are made in a particular order. You first check all the comparisons made with the smallest mean (starting with the comparison between smallest and largest, then smallest and second largest and so on). Next check all comparisons with the second smallest (starting with the comparison between it and the largest as before). When you are checking comparisons for a given mean (e.g. the second smallest) you stop checking further comparisons with that mean as soon as any are found that are not significant. Thus, when you are checking comparisons for a mean such as the second smallest, you are starting with the largest difference (because you first compare it with the largest mean and then descend through the others in order). If you come to one that is not significant, forget the remaining comparisons and start looking at the comparisons for the third smallest. Continue in this way until all comparisons are either checked or skipped because a preceding comparison with the same mean was not significant. This sounds horrendous but it is simpler than it sounds. It is repetitive rather than difficult. In our example, the rank ordering of means is A,B,C. We therefore start by comparing A and C. If this is significant, then test A and B. Finally do B and C.

The Newman–Keuls test can be useful if you need a sensitive test and your groups have equal numbers. The aim of a *post hoc* procedure like this is to ensure that each comparison you make is made at the α-level you choose. In other words, to make certain the chances of a type I error are held at .05 for each comparison. However, statisticians now argue that the Newman–Keuls test fails to do this — it is a bit too generous in some circumstances. If you need to be very careful to avoid promiscuously declaring a difference significant, avoid this test.

8.5.5 The Scheffé test

This is a conservative procedure, but a flexible one. It can cope with unequal group sizes, and so allows also for comparisons of the type 'A against B and C taken together' described above. This test uses an *F*-ratio.

$$F = \frac{(\overline{M}_1 - \overline{M}_2)^2}{\frac{\text{error}}{n_1} + \frac{\text{error}}{n_2}}$$

This value is calculated for each comparison required. The error term used is, as before, the error term used to test the corresponding main effect in the overall ANOVA. The *F* calculated here has $(k{-}1, N{-}k)$ degrees of freedom, where k is the number of levels of the factor within which the comparisons are being made, and $N{-}k$ is the degrees of freedom associated with the error MS. The obtained value of *F* is compared with a critical value of *F*.

The critical value is calculated by looking up *F*-tables as usual with $df = (k{-}1, N{-}k)$, and then multiplying the value found by $k{-}1$. This is strict, and will lead to fewer significant differences than most of the other tests discussed here. Scheffé himself suggested that it might often be reasonable to use the .1 α-level because his test is so tight.

To make contrasts of the more general type we mentioned, such as 'A against B and C taken together', just set M_1 and n_1 to values appropriate for A, but set M_2 and n_2 to the mean and n obtained from the group created by combining B and C.

8.6   CHOOSING A PROCEDURE

We have listed a number of different approaches to making specific comparisons among groups. In practice, you probably only need one or perhaps two of these techniques. You will naturally be asking which is most appropriate for your application. This is a question that statisticians debate and so there is no single correct answer. However, it is possible to provide some rules of thumb. First, if your comparisons are planned and there are relatively few of them, then tests using unadjusted significance levels are sensible. If you are carrying out many planned comparisons or a few *post hoc* comparisons then the Bonferroni adjustment to the significance level is appropriate. The Bonferroni approach is the most flexible of the approaches described, is easy to carry out and would only rarely be a poor choice. If, however, you decide, having seen the data, that you want to test all pairwise comparisons of means, then Tukey's test is better than the Bonferroni approach.

The four procedures described allow for the size of the set of comparisons being made when the problem of multiplicity arises. They adjust the criterion for significance so that the hurdle is higher when more comparisons are made. They vary in the way they do this and so different tests vary in the strictness of the criterion. A separate issue arises for the researcher, which is to decide which comparisons should be taken as a set. All comparisons in the same set need to be taken into account, but this set can be defined narrowly or widely. A wide definition of the set would be, say, all the comparisons you might make in a given project. This definition will give a large number of comparisons and so will produce a very strict criterion for significance. On the other hand, it would let you be confident that anything that did meet the criterion really was significant at the chosen level. However, researchers usually choose to define the set narrowly. They group tests into subsets. Each subset consists of the comparisons associated with a given term in the original statistical model. For example, in a two-way ANOVA there are three terms (two main effects and one interaction). Adjustments to critical values are made separately for each term. If you compared the means for groups at different levels of one predictor variable, you would take into account only the number of comparisons made among levels of that variable. This provides more generous criteria for significance than if you took into account comparisons for the other terms as well. These subsets of comparisons are termed families of comparisons and this approach is referred to as controlling the familywise error rate. A wider approach, which takes into account all the comparisons in an entire experiment would control the experimentwise error rate.

Multiple comparison procedures aim to control the significance level so that the report a researcher makes is accurate. If these adjustments are not made, the actual significance level can be substantially different from the superficial level. As we have noted, the relative merit of different procedures remains a matter for debate among statisticians. It is important when weighing their merits to consider what conclusion you might draw from the comparison. *Post hoc* tests, in particular, are essentially a type of EDA. A large difference between two conditions which becomes apparent only once the data have been gathered and which was not intially a focus of the study can be regarded in the same way as an anomalous pattern in the residuals. It is a potentially interesting observation which may be worth following up in a fresh study. Although you may be able to draw interesting conclusions from it immediately, you are likely to wish to test its reliability through replication. In this event, deriving a precise significance level is not a central issue. On the other hand, to the extent that you wish to draw definitive conclusions from the data to hand, precise control over significance levels will be important.

8.7 POLYNOMIAL CONTRASTS

Frequently you will be interested in a pattern across the levels of a factor that does not simply involve pairwise comparisons. For example, if the levels of a factor correspond to levels of illumination, and your dependent variable is the time taken to name an object, then you might predict that the time to name the object will grow steadily shorter as the level of illumination rises. One way to test this hypothesis is to test a linear trend. If three levels of brightness were used in the study, then you could use this contrast:

Contrast $= -1\ 0 + 1$

If there were, say, five levels, then you would need a contrast with five elements:

Contrast $= -2 - 1\ 0 + 1 + 2$

Each of these contrasts describes the same form of relationship: a steady increase across the levels of the factor. Another kind of pattern that you might want to test for is a u-shaped curve across the levels of a factor. This is called a quadratic trend. For example, the relationship between anxiety and performance depicted in Fig 5.3 is a quadratic relationship. Coefficients to test this would be, for instance:

Contrast $= 1 - 1 - 1\ 1$

There are other shapes of curves that you can test against the levels of your factor.

8.8 CONTRASTS WITHIN AN INTERACTION

When a significant interaction is found, it is often interesting to nail down the pattern of differences. As we saw in Chapter 4, the first step is to obtain the relevant cell means and display them. Either a table or a plot can be used, and plots such as the one in Fig 4.4 are frequently used in journal articles. By inspecting the means, you can see the relationships among different conditions that give rise to the interaction. It is then appropriate to test whether the differences detected by eye are statistically significant. Two approaches to this are common.

8.8.1 Simple main effects

The first approach tests simple main effects of one variable at each level of the other. To illustrate this, we will use the example from Schachter's study of the relationship between obesity and appetite that we first examined in Chapter 4. The cell means are reproduced in Table 8.1.

Table 8.1   Cell means for obesity study

	Normal weight	Obese
Recently fed	1.50	3.83
Starved	4.33	3.83

The interaction of weight and hunger was statistically significant, $F(1, 20) = 14.21$, $p < .01$. This means that, say, the effect of hunger is not the same at each level of weight. Simple main effects test whether the effect of one predictor is significant separately at each level of the other. A test of the simple main effects of hunger, for example, tests the effect of hunger at each level of weight. For this data, you would expect that the effect of hunger with the normal weight group is significant, while with the obese group there would be no difference between the fed and starved groups.

You can think of each test of a simple main effect as being like a one-way ANOVA. For example, the simple main effect of hunger for obese subjects is like a one-way ANOVA comparing obese participants who had been fed with obese subjects who were hungry. The test will use as the numerator of an *F*-ratio the between-groups variance based on these two cells only. The denominator may be based on within-groups variance estimated from these cells only. In this case the test is exactly the same as a one-way ANOVA. However, if the assumption of homogeneity of variance described in Chapter 3 is satisfied, then a better estimate of error variance can be obtained by basing it on all four cells in the design. This is the error variance derived from the original factorial analysis of variance and may allow a more powerful test.

8.8.2 Comparing cell means

In this example, there are only two levels of each factor, and so it is unlikely to be fruitful to analyse the cell means further. However, you will often want to make specific comparisons between pairs of cell means. For example, you might want to test whether the difference between fed and starved groups was significant for normal weight participants. Of course, in this example these are the only two levels and so the simple main effect answers the question. However, when you do want to compare cell means in a between-subjects design, use an ordinary *t*-test, taking as the error term the error from the ANOVA. You can test this for significance using a critical value determined by the Bonferroni approach.

It should be noted that contrasts of cell means do not test the same hypotheses as the interaction term in the ANOVA. Contrasts between cell means are influenced by main effects as well as the interaction. This means, for example, that it is possible to find that the interaction is significant but no comparison of cell means is significant. Rosenthal and Rosnow (1985) argue in favour of not testing cell means, but instead directly testing components of the interaction term. However, it is usually easier to understand and interpret contrasts between cell means.

8.9 CONTRASTS WITH REPEATED MEASURES

It is common in psychological research for the same participants to be observed under more than one condition. That is, data in different cells can come from the same subjects. The appropriate way to calculate specific contrasts is affected by this. In general, statistical software may not provide the appropriate statistics. For a one-way repeated measures ANOVA, the appropriate method is the Bonferroni procedure. This is also appropriate for contrasts among the levels of a within-subjects variable in a factorial design. The only difference from the procedure described above is that now the *t*-test for repeated measures should be used. The formula for this is:

$$ t = \frac{M_1 - M_2}{\frac{SD_{diff}}{\sqrt{n}}} $$

Where SD_{diff} is the standard deviation of the differences between participants' scores in the two conditions.

Designs with both repeated measures and between-groups variables are frequent in psychology. For example, different ages of children might be tested on their ability to perform different kinds of arithmetic problem. The different arithmetic problems could be a repeated measures variable, with every participant attempting each kind of problem. Specific comparisons on between-group variables in such designs, the age groups in this example, can be made in the same way as for ordinary between-groups studies using any of the tests mentioned above. Comparisons among means for within subjects variables should use the Bonferroni approach with a repeated measures *t*-test.

As with between-groups designs, you may be interested to test specific contrasts among the cells defined by a design. This can be a useful follow-up to a significant interaction effect in the ANOVA or may be a planned contrast. Simple main effects are calculated by running a one-way ANOVA that ignores the other levels of the variable. When you investigate the simple main effects of a repeated measures variable, remember to use the repeated measures ANOVA to test it.

Comparisons of cell means can be of one of two types. Either they compare subjects in the different groups at each level of the repeated measures variable, or they compare performance in the different conditions separately for each group. The former uses an ordinary *t*-test, with Bonferroni adjustment. The latter again uses the Bonferroni approach with a repeated measures *t*-test.

Many textbooks describe alternative procedures for pairwise comparisons and tests of simple main effects in a repeated measures design. The alternative procedures use what is called a pooled estimate of error variance. The methods that I have described base the estimate of error variance just on the cells being contrasted. Procedures that use a pooled estimate base it on the cells being contrasted and other cells in the design. The advantage of a pooled estimate is that because the estimate is based on more data points, it will have more degrees of freedom and so a more lenient critical value will be available. The disadvantage is that you are relying on the assumption of homogeneity of variance being satisfied. That is, pooling variances across cells does assume that they are all estimates of the same population value. For many practical situations, the assumption is not satisfied. When it is not satisfied, the comparisons will sometimes be too lenient, sometimes too strict, but you will not know which. I recommend instead following procedures that do not use pooled estimates of variance. These will sometimes be too strict, especially if the homogeneity of variance assumption is satisfied, but at least the direction of bias is consistent. Furthermore, you can check for homogeneity of variance and if you find that it is satisfied, you can take that into account when you interpret the results of the test.

When you contrast cell means, you need to think about the interpretation you will make of any difference you find. If your tests are *post hoc* but you really do want to interpret the results as definitive tests of some hypothesis, then you must at least employ conservative critical values. On the other hand, if you regard the *post hoc* tests as suggestive, as indications of promising avenues for further investigation, then it is sensible to take a more liberal approach.

8.10 SUMMARY

In many circumstances, ANOVA will not provide specific tests of the questions you actually want to answer. Specific comparisons can be carried out to test differences between pairs of means, and more general patterns across the levels of an explanatory variable can be tested using contrast coefficients. When problems of multiplicity arise, either because you carry out several tests or because you select comparisons *post hoc*, you need to use procedures that conserve p-values. However, when *post hoc* comparisons are exploratory, and are interpreted as exploratory, it may be useful to take a more relaxed view of p-values.

9 MODEL COMPARISON

For the most part we have so far considered situations where you design a model and fit it to the data. The quality of the fit is used to determine whether the model is accepted. In these examples, just one model has been considered and tested. This is an excellent way of thinking about data analysis. However, there is a more general way of approaching statistical modelling. This is the model comparison approach. In model comparison, statistical testing is carried out by comparing two models.

This chapter explains the model comparison approach and illustrates the way it is applied to multiple regression. In the next chapter, we will see how it is applied to log-linear analysis.

Two models can be compared in terms of the amount of variance they account for. The more variance a model can account for, the better it fits the data. If one model accounts for more variance than another model, then it is, all other things being equal, a better model. The difference in the amount of variance two models account for can be estimated and tested for statistical significance.

Model comparison can be used to evaluate individual predictors. One way of testing whether a predictor variable is significant is to compare two models which differ in that the first does not include the predictor but the second does. If the predictor accounts for a significant amount of additional variance, then the second model will account for significantly more variance than the first. This simple idea is tremendously powerful. However, to understand this kind of analysis, you need to understand the difference between the unique variance that a predictor accounts for and the total variance it accounts for.

The total variance that a predictor accounts for is the square of the correlation between that predictor and the outcome variable. This encompasses the whole relationship between the predictor and the outcome.

The unique variance that can be attributed to a predictor is the influence it has on the outcome after the influence of other predictor variables has been taken into account. The unique variance is dependent, then, on which other predictors are taken into account. Unique variance is what standard multiple regression tests. As we saw in the chapter on multiple regression, the size of regression coefficients for each predictor will depend on which other predictors are included in the model.

In standard multiple regression, as we saw in an earlier chapter, the coefficients can be used to test the unique variance explained by each predictor. This unique variance is the squared semi-partial correlation, sr^2. It is the variance in the outcome variable that is explained by a given predictor alone. As we saw, it will depend on which other predictors are in the model. If predictors overlap, as they often will, then the variance they share reduces their unique effects. The unique effect of a predictor is its correlation with the outcome less any overlap. Thus the unique effect of a given predictor in multiple regression depends on which other predictors are included in the model.

One limitation of standard multiple regression is that overlap variance is not attributed to any of the predictors in the model. This means that frequently the total of the sr^2 values for individual predictors is less than the R^2 for the overall model. The overall R^2 includes both individual sr^2 values and overlap variance. Hierarchical regression offers a mechanism by which overlap variance can be assigned to particular predictors.

9.1   HIERARCHICAL MULTIPLE REGRESSION

Standard multiple regression produces a measure of the amount of variance the model fitted accounts for. This is called squared multiple R (R^2) and represents the proportion of variability in the dependent variable that can be explained by the predictor variables. The significance test for a model compares variance explained to error variance using an F-ratio. As I noted in Chapter 5 you will almost always find that this is significant.

However, you can compare two models in a similar way. You use the difference in the amount of variance the two models account for as the numerator of an F-ratio. If this difference is large compared to error variance, then it may be statistically significant. The precise details of an appropriate formula will be given below.

This method is used in an approach to data analysis called hierarchical multiple regression. Hierarchical regression involves building a sequence of several models. Models in the sequence contain additional predictor variables. If the extra explanatory variable that is added to the model makes a significant additional contribution towards accounting for differences in scores, then it will increase R^2 significantly.

This method differs from standard multiple regression in the way overlap variance is assigned to predictors. In standard multiple regression, overlap variance is not assigned to any predictor. Each predictor is attributed with only the unique variance it can explain. Overlap variance is discarded. In hierarchical multiple regression, variables included first are assigned the overlap variance. Therefore, overlap variance can be assigned to one predictor rather than another by selecting which should be given priority in the model.

For example, in the study of conceptual knowledge, there is debate as to why some properties are more central to concepts than others. For instance, the property of having fur may be more central to the concept of a cat than having a tail. Ratings of centrality can be gathered by asking subjects to imagine a cat without, say, fur and recording how good an example of a cat this cat without fur would be. This experiment was carried out by Schunn and Vera (1995). In their study, they wanted to test alternative explanations of why some properties are more central than others. In one experiment, they got subjects to rank properties according to their importance for (a) people recognizing cats and (b) cats functioning successfully as cats. They expected that if properties were central to a concept because they were important in recognizing objects, then ranks for each property in condition (a) would correlate highly with their centrality ratings. Similarly, if properties were central because of their functional or causal role, then ranks in (b) would correlate well with centrality ratings.

Schunn and Vera report the correlations among variables shown in Table 9.1. From these, I have calculated the percentage of variance in centrality accounted for by the predictor variables. The sr^2 for recognition is 7.6%, the sr^2 for function is 10%, and the overlap is 27.2%.

Notice that for each predictor the sum of overlap variance and unique variance is equal to the square of the simple bivariate correlation between that predictor and the outcome variable. In other words, the total variance that each explains is split between unique variance and overlap variance.

In standard multiple regression, each variable is assigned only its unique variance. In hierarchical regression, the first variable included in the model will grab the overlap variance as well. For example, if you first build the model M9.1, then *function* will be assigned the whole of the variance it shares with the outcome.

M9.1: centrality = constant + function + error

In hierarchical regression, M9.1 is then compared with M9.2 to see whether *recognition* has any influence on *centrality* over and above the

Table 9.1 Correlations between centrality ratings and different kinds of property

	Centrality	Recognition	Function
Centrality	—		
Recognition	0.59	—	
Function	0.61	0.61	—

effect of *function*. The difference between M9.1 and M9.2 provides a test of any remaining effect of *recognition* once *function* has been taken into account.

M9.2: centrality = constant + function + recognition + error

You can imagine building up a regression equation, step-by-step, adding one additional predictor at a time. Each predictor added absorbs a little more variance. Each can be tested in turn to see whether it is significant.

9.2   PREDICTOR VARIABLES THAT OVERLAP

In a simple world, the bits of variance accounted for by successive predictors would stack up like slices of cake. Each predictor would have its own distinct slice. It would not matter in which order they came to the table, the same amount of cake would be waiting for them. The different slices could simply be added up to calculate the total variance accounted for by any given model.

This additive view is, however, only correct if each predictor you consider is independent of the others. For multiple regression problems this is often not true. If the predictors are correlated with one another, then they are competing for the same slice of variance. The amount of variance attributed to a particular predictor will depend on which other predictors were included in the model. This makes interpreting a comparison between two models more complex.

Analysis of variance models are built on the assumption that the factors in the model are independent. The factors in ANOVA correspond to predictors in multiple regression. These factors have additive effects and the variance can be neatly sliced up, or partitioned. The factors are said to be orthogonal.

However, in multiple regression, the order in which terms enter the model affects the proportion of variance that gets attributed to each. Here, the predictors are like sponges being dunked in a mug of coffee. Each soaks up some variance. In hierarchical multiple regression, the first sponge dropped in gets first crack at the variance. It is greedy and soaks up all it can. If two predictors are correlated, the variance they can account for overlaps. If one predictor enters the model first, it soaks up the area of overlap for itself and the overlap is not shared.

In standard multiple regression, the predictors all enter the model simultaneously. This is like throwing the sponges into your coffee together. They share overlapping variance. In this situation, the squared semi-partial correlation (sr^2) corresponds to the regression coefficient. They test the same thing: the unique variance excluding any overlap with other predictors in the model. Thus the t-test printed out with the multiple regression results for each coefficient is a test of the statistical significance of sr^2. However, in hierarchical or stepwise regression, sr^2 no longer corresponds to the regression coefficient, but the t-test does still test the regression coefficient. To evaluate whether sr^2 is significant, you need to compare the models.

Comparison of models is done by fitting first a model including all the predictors except for the one you want to test. You then add the ones you want to test, and see how the fit improves. For example, to account for rates of offending using the data described briefly in Chapter 6, you might look at the effect of adding the variables movies and sport to a model which already included IQ and adjustment. This would involve comparing (a) with (b):

(a) record = constant + IQ + adjustment + error
(b) record = constant + IQ + adjustment + movies + sport + error

To evaluate whether (b) accounts for significantly more variance than (a), you test whether the difference in the variance the respective models account for is large compared to error. Here is an appropriate formula (Tabachnik and Fidell, 1989).

$$F_{\text{inc}} = \frac{(R^2_b - R^2_a)/M}{(1 + R^2_b)/\text{df}_{\text{error}}}$$

Where:
M is the number of predictors added (two in the example)
R^2_b is the squared multiple R for the more inclusive model
R^2_a is the squared multiple R for the less inclusive model
df_{error} is the degrees of freedom for the error term in the more inclusive model

9.3 ANOVA AS MODEL COMPARISON

The model comparison approach can be employed quite generally as a way of thinking about all model fitting (Maxwell and Delaney, 1990). For example, one-way ANOVA can be thought of as a model comparison. I have talked about one-way ANOVA as fitting the model M9.3 to data.

M9.3: score = constant + predictor + error

The variance is partitioned into variance attributable to the explanatory variable and variance attributed to *error*. If the former is large compared to the latter, the influence of the predictor may be significant. It is possible to view this instead as the comparison of two models. The first model is M9.3 as just described. The second is called a restricted model. In this model, the effect of the predictor is fixed at zero. For this example, the restricted model would be M9.4.

M9.4: score = constant + error

The test, then, is whether the difference in variance accounted for by M9.3 and M9.4 is large compared to *error*. This is just a different way of describing the same process of fitting a model to data.

9.4   SUMMARY

The effect of an explanatory variable can be evaluated by comparing a model which includes it to one that does not. The resulting change in quality of fit can be used to assess the effect of the variable.

10 LOG-LINEAR ANALYSIS

Some observations are very simple. For example, you might observe whether it is raining or the sun is shining. There is no ruler you can stretch between rain and sunshine. They just are different things. Nevertheless, the observation might be important. There are lots of examples of observations that simply distinguish between two distinct types or categories. For example, you might observe whether a participant is male or female, whether they are religious or a non-believer, whether they are a lawyer or a milkman, whether their sweater is red or blue. All of these are categorical distinctions.

In ANOVA, all the variables except the outcome are categorical. Each explanatory variable makes a division into categories. In multiple regression, the outcome and possibly all of the predictors are continuous rather than categorical. In log-linear analysis, all of the variables are categorical, including the outcome.

Categorical analyses are particularly appropriate in two areas of psychology. First, there are studies which have a sociological foundation. They are concerned to understand behaviour in terms of the ways people are grouped in society. For example, are men or women, the old or the young, black or white, more likely to vote for the left or the right? Second, studies involving children frequently employ success or failure on a task as a measure. The child is either able to perform successfully or not. In these areas of psychology, log-linear analysis can be a useful tool.

Log-linear analysis works in a similar way to hierarchical regression. The various predictors that could account for an outcome are added to a model in turn and their effectiveness in explaining variation in the outcome is compared. The main difference is that in log-linear analysis the model predicts the relative frequency of different outcomes.

10.1 PEARSON CHI-SQUARE

Before illustrating log-linear analysis, it is worth mentioning that there are other statistics that can be used with this kind of data. The most

Table 10.1 Political affiliations of men
and women

	Left wing	Right wing
Men	33	27
Women	28	32

familiar is undoubtedly the Pearson chi-square statistic. For example, if
you want to know whether the sex of a voter helps to explain whether
they prefer to vote for a party on the right or left of the political
spectrum, you could ask a sample of men and women which way they
prefer to vote. Table 10.1 contains some imaginary data.

The Pearson chi-square can be used to answer the question whether
the distribution of voters to the left and right is independent of their sex.
If sex influences voting behaviour, then it will not be independent. The
number of people in the left and right categories will depend on whether
you look at the male row or the female row. The Pearson chi-square
works by comparing the distribution of cases that is observed in the data
to the distribution you would expect to see if sex and voting are
independent. If these distributions are similar, and the observed data is
quite like the data you would expect if they were independent, then you
have no evidence that they are related. On the other hand, if there is a
large difference, then you conclude that sex and voting are not
independent.

There are two key steps. First, you must work out what the expected
frequencies are. Second, you must calculate how far they diverge from
the frequencies observed. The expected frequency is usually derived by
assuming that if the two variables are independent, then the cases will be
distributed in similar proportions across the categories. A simple formula
is used to calculate the expected frequencies for each cell in the table.

Expected frequency = (row total * column total)/total number of cases

For example, the expected frequency of male left-wingers is

Expected = (number of men * number of left-wingers)/total
          = (60 * 61)/120
          = 30.5

The second step is to calculate how far these expected frequencies
diverge from the frequencies observed. For men voting for a party of the
left, the expected frequency is 30.5, the observed frequency is 33, and so
the difference is 2.5. The formula for the Pearson chi-square simply
squares the difference for each cell, divides by the expected frequency for
that cell, and then sums these values across cells. For the voting
behaviour example, the three panels of Table 10.2 illustrate this.

Table 10.2 Calculation of Pearson chi-square

	Expected (E)		Difference (D)		D^2/E	
	Left	Right	Left	Right	Left	Right
Men	30.5	29.5	2.5	2.5	0.205	0.212
Women	30.5	29.5	2.5	2.5	0.205	0.212

The values in the cells of the final table are summed to give χ^2, which can be assessed against tables of critical values. The larger the value of χ^2, the greater the difference between the model and the observed data. If χ^2 is significant, then the model, that sex and voting behaviour are independent, is unlikely to have produced the observed data. For our example:

$$\chi^2 = 0.205 + 0.212 + 0.205 + 0.212 = 0.834, \, p > 0.2, \text{ not significant}$$

Although there are discrepancies between the model and the data, they can be attributed to chance. You would conclude that sex does not influence voting. In this example, the model provides a good fit to the data.

Notice here the negative strategy for hypothesis testing. To test the hypothesis that sex influences voting, you try to show that a model which assumes that sex and voting are independent cannot account for the data. If it can, your hypothesis is rejected.

10.2 MORE THAN TWO VARIABLES

The Pearson chi-square has a limitation. It cannot be readily generalized to problems where there are additional predictor variables. This contrasts with ANOVA. ANOVA can be used with just one predictor variable, but it can be generalized to any number of predictors. For example, if you want to look at the influence of sex, age and education on voting behaviour, with ANOVA you can build a model that incorporates all three predictors and their interactions. With the Pearson chi-square, you would have to do three separate analyses for the three predictors.

It would be tempting, then, to use ANOVA to test categorical data. But this is not appropriate (with one exception, which I return to shortly) because in general categorical data violates assumptions of ANOVA. For example, if you are studying the relationship between the animals people keep as companions and their own occupation, you might gather data like that displayed in Table 10.3.

The two dimensions being looked at are the kind of pet and the occupation. But these dimensions are not like the scales used as dependent variables in ANOVA, such as response time. Two response times can

Table 10.3   Categorical data

	Cat	Dog	Goldfish	Parrot	Mouse
Farmer	12	15	5	—	—
Lawyer	9	8	7	1	2
Engineer	5	10	3	—	—

be compared and you can meaningfully say that one is 'more' than the other. There is no obvious way in which you can say that a goldfish is more than a bird. The kind of pet someone chooses is a categorical or nominal variable. All you have to be able to do is classify the pets (i.e. be able to judge equality). In contrast, two response times can be compared and you can say, for example, that a time of 400 ms is less than a time of 500 ms. Moreover, if time A is greater than time B, and B is greater than C, then you can be sure that A is greater than C. This relation is called transitivity. Thus response time is at least an ordinal variable. In addition, we generally accept that the difference between 400 and 500 ms is equal to the difference between 700 and 800 ms. The same numerical interval is equivalent at different places on the scale. This makes response time an interval variable. To satisfy the assumptions of ANOVA, a measurement should be made on an interval scale, or at least a scale which can be treated as an interval scale. In short, the categorization of pets is not an appropriate variable for ANOVA. The computations performed during ANOVA imply that data has been measured on an interval scale.

There is one exception to this, which it is useful to be aware of. Many statisticians argue that ANOVA can be used with a categorical dependent variable that uses just two categories and where the proportion of cases in either category is not more than .8. For example, if people's pets are classified as warm versus cold blooded, just two categories are used. Where you use ANOVA with a dichotomous variable, you arbitrarily allocate one category the value 1, and the other is scored as zero.

Log-linear analysis provides a method for testing categorical data by building models that can accommodate several predictors. Like ANOVA, it provides a way of breaking down variation in the outcome variable into component effects. Parts of the variation in outcome are attributed to each predictor, and tests can be made of the significance of each effect.

10.3   HIERARCHICAL ANALYSIS OF MODELS

At the beginning of this chapter, we noted that log-linear analysis works like hierarchical regression, in that a model is built by adding one predictor at a time and evaluating the contribution it makes to accounting for the data. This is done by examining how well the model that includes it fits the data compared to a model that leaves it out.

Log-linear analysis also has similarities to the Pearson chi-square. Log-linear analysis uses the same key steps as the Pearson chi-square to evaluate a model. First, expected frequencies are calculated. These expected frequencies reflect the model. Second, the magnitude of the difference between these expected frequencies and the frequencies observed is calculated. The main difference is that a different formula is used to calculate the quality of the fit. Log-linear analysis uses the likelihood ratio chi-square.

Thus, log-linear analysis proceeds by evaluating a series of models. At each step, the model is used to work out expected frequencies, and these are compared to the observed frequencies using the likelihood ratio chi-square. If the model fits the data well, then the discrepancy will be small and the likelihood ratio chi-square will not be significant. Adjacent steps in the series contrast models which differ in that one includes a predictor which the next leaves out. The significance of this predictor can be evaluated by testing the difference in the quality of fit of the two models. If there is a large difference, then this predictor is making a large contribution towards accounting for the data.

For example, if you investigated the relationship between sex (man or woman) and age (old or young) in relation to voting behaviour, your data would be laid out as a three-way table (Table 10.4). You would decide on a series of models to test. You might look at these:

M10.1: $\log(f)$ = party + age + sex
M10.2: $\log(f)$ = party + age + sex + age * sex
M10.3: $\log(f)$ = party + age + sex + age * sex + age * party
M10.4: $\log(f)$ = party + age + sex + age * sex + age * party + sex * party
M10.5: $\log(f)$ = party + age + sex + age * sex + age * party
$\qquad$ + sex * party + age * sex * party

At each step, the models differ in that one additional effect has been added. The significance of that effect can be evaluated by examining the change in the likelihood ratio chi-square between steps. You select models that allow you to test effects that are of interest.

The likelihood ratio chi-square is calculated using the following formula.

Table 10.4 Three-way design with categorical data

	Left wing		Right wing	
	Old	Young	Old	Young
Men				
Women				

Table 10.5   Calculation of likelihood-ratio chi-square

	Expected (E)		log obs − log exp		*obs	
	Left	Right	Left	Right	Left	Right
Men	30.5	29.5	0.079	−0.089	2.600	−2.391
Women	30.5	29.5	−0.086	0.081	−2.395	2.603

$$G^2 = 2 \sum (\text{observed} * (\text{log observed} - \text{log expected}))$$

This can be applied to the two-way table for which we calculated the Pearson chi-square earlier. For each cell, (log observed − log expected) is first calculated. Then this difference is multiplied by the observed frequency for that cell. These values are then summed and the total is doubled to yield G^2. This is illustrated in Table 10.5.

$$G^2 = 2 * (2.600 - 2.391 - 2.395 + 2.603) = 0.834$$

G^2 is checked against the same critical values as χ^2. As is the case in this example, the two statistics usually give similar results. The crucial distinction is that the difference between two G^2 values is a G^2, and so can be evaluated for significance. This allows you to test the effect of a predictor by adding it to a model and evaluating the change in G^2. You just subtract the G^2 for one model from the G^2 for the other and see if the difference exceeds the critical value for G^2. This is not the case for χ^2.

    The role of logarithms may be a little puzzling, but you can think of them as just a way of transforming the data so that the assumptions of a useful statistic are met. Log-linear models estimate the logarithm of cell frequencies rather than the frequencies themselves.

    At each step in the hierarchical series, an additional effect is added to the model. Adding another effect changes the expected frequencies. It provides a further condition that they must take into account. This is most easily illustrated with a simple example. Earlier, we calculated estimated frequencies for the two-way table relating sex and voting behaviour. The estimates took into account both the relative numbers of men and women and the relative numbers of left and right wingers. In other words, both variables were in the model. However, a simple model could be constructed with only sex as a variable. Now only the relative number of men and women is taken into account. The different proportions of left and right wing people are not taken into account. In this case, there is the same number of men as women, and so the estimate is simply that there will be the same frequency in every cell.

    With new expected frequencies, the likelihood ratio chi-square is recalculated for the new model. This is illustrated in Table 10.6. The resulting value for G^2 is 0.866. The effect of politics can be estimated as

Table 10.6 Likehood ratio chi-square taking into account constraints from the row variable only

	Expected (E)		log obs − log exp		*obs	
	Left	Right	Left	Right	Left	Right
Men	30	30	0.095	−0.105	3.145	−2.845
Women	30	30	−0.069	0.065	−1.932	2.065

Table 10.7 Hierarchical analysis

Model	G^2	Effect deleted	ΔG^2
Sex + politics	0.834		
Sex	0.866	Politics	0.032

the difference between values for the two successive steps. This is illustrated in Table 10.7. The ΔG^2 value in Table 10.7 indicates the extent to which the fit of the model is improved by taking into account the influence of the politics effect over and above the effect of sex.

For each data set, there is one model which accounts exactly for the frequencies as they are observed. This model is called the saturated model. Every constraint on the frequencies is taken into account when the estimates are derived. For the two-way table, these constraints would be the effect of sex, the effect of voting, and finally the different effect on voting of each gender. That is, every possible effect. The saturated model estimates that the frequency in each cell will be the observed frequency. Naturally, the saturated model fits perfectly. It has zero degrees of freedom, because every constraint on the data has been employed, and the value of G^2 is 0 because there is no difference between the values estimated and those observed.

10.4 SUMMARY

When you want to analyse categorical data, log-linear analysis allows you to examine the effects of several variables and their interactions. Log-linear analysis assesses each term by measuring the difference it makes to the quality of the model. The likelihood ratio chi-square is used to calculate the fit of the model at each step. The difference between values of this statistic are compared because the differences between likelihood ratio chi-squares themselves follow a chi-square distribution, and so their statistical significance can be found.

11 RELIABILITY

Psychological testing occurs widely, being used particularly in personnel selection, in clinical settings and in education. The decisions that test results influence can have a large effect on the applicant, the patient, the student, your client. It is a matter of considerable ethical and practical importance to be sure we use tests appropriately, and that tests are constructed to be accurate and fair.

Tests are often used in research, too. For example, you might want to conduct an experiment comparing the reaction times of subjects with different body image scores in a lexical decision task using nouns denoting foodstuffs as the target items. You could use each subject's score on a body image questionnaire to separate subjects into groups, for example. In the experimental setting, the ethical issues are a little different. Your use of the score is unlikely to have a great effect on subjects' futures. Nevertheless, it is crucial to the interpretation of your experiment that the questionnaire used is genuinely measuring the variable of interest.

Test construction is an industry. There are many standard tests available which have been carefully tested and standardized. Nevertheless, you should not just take the test publisher at his word. Weigh up whether a given test is suitable for your application. If you want to make up a new test (perhaps there does not seem to be any published test that meets your needs), be aware that constructing a new test is a project in itself! That is definitely not intended to discourage you from taking on a test construction project. Test construction done properly can make a really good project. In this chapter, we will look at the basic techniques used for checking the reliability of a test, the principal ways scores from a test can be presented, and the main forms of interpretation of tests.

11.1   TEST SCORES

After running a test, you end up with raw scores. Each subject takes the test, and different subjects get different scores. However, raw scores are difficult to interpret.

First, it is hard to compare raw scores from different tests. If David scores 27 on his Body Image test, and 14 on the Embedded Figures Test (EFT), what does it tell us about his relative scores on the two tests? Is his body image 'better' than his perceptual skill?

Second, it is not straightforward to compare participants' relative performance on different tests. For example, if Sally got 18 and Harry got 9 on the EFT, is Sally twice as good as Harry? The answer is that it depends on the items included in the test. If the first nine items are really easy, just a warm up, and each item from 10 to 20 adds increasing difficulty, then Sally might be several times as good as Harry. On the other hand, if the easiest item represents a fairly high level of ability, and the other items make fairly fine differentiations, then the difference between Harry and Sally may be quite small.

What is needed is a way to convert scores from different tests to some common scale so that we can compare them meaningfully. There are two principal ways of getting round these problems. The scores can be converted to either percentiles or to standard scores. Percentiles and standard scores are two ways of presenting scores so that they are easy to interpret. The raw scores for a small group of subjects (including Sally, Harry and David) are shown in Table 11.1.

A percentile score indicates the standing of a subject in relation to the other subjects tested. A subject with a percentile score of 10 stands above 10% of the group. A percentile score of 90 puts a subject above 90% of the group. The procedure for calculating percentiles is slightly tedious, so I will not repeat it in detail here. Essentially, it involves constructing a cumulative frequency distribution. This distribution indicates how many other scores fall below each score. This number is converted to a proportion of the total number of scores, and this is used to calculate the percentile. The 50th percentile, of course, is the median.

Percentiles have a drawback that has diminished their popularity as a technique for score conversion. Scores near the middle of the range are separated more strongly than extreme scores. This is because there are more scores in the middle of the range. A small increase in a subject's raw score near the middle can raise her past other subjects with similar

Table 11.1   Test data

Name	EFT	Body image
S	18	24
H	9	12
D	14	27
Sh	16	23
R	7	36
T	19	31
F	6	22

scores and can therefore lead to a noticeable increase in her percentile. If, on the other hand, a subject has a very high score, an increase of several marks may not change her relative standing, only because there are few other people at the extremes of the range.

It is not appropriate to use percentiles as input to a parametric statistical test, because they are not normally distributed.

Standard scores translate raw performance into an indication of relative standing. A good example of a standard score is the z-score. The z-score indicates how many standard deviations a score is from the mean. Thus, a subject getting a z-score of 3 is pretty good because it is three standard deviations better than the average. The z-score for an observation is calculated by dividing the difference between the score and the mean by the standard deviation (SD).

$$z\text{-score}_i = (\text{score}_i - \text{mean})/SD$$

Table 11.2 displays the standard scores for the data in Table 11.1.

The distributions of the z-scores show that although Sally's scores are higher than Harry's on both tests, this difference needs to be interpreted differently in each case. Sally has a relatively high z-score for the EFT, but Harry's is clearly not too far from the middle of the sample. Harry and Sally are, however, both below average on the Body Image test. Sally is close to the average, but Harry's score is unusually low. Note that David's score is almost exactly the same on the two tests when it is converted to a z-score (though the raw score for one test is almost double his raw score on the other).

Both z-scores and percentiles allow us to interpret test results in relation to the distribution of scores in the sample. They give us a standard frame of reference for the interpretation of scores. Some tests give results that are ready-standardized. For example, many tests of general intellectual ability (IQ tests) produce scores standardized on a mean of 100 and an SD of 15. This standardization is done by the constructors of the test, who try the test out on a large sample of subjects. The raw scores for this sample are converted so that their mean is 100

Table 11.2 Test data standardized

Name	EFT standardized	Body image standardized
S	0.989	−0.132
H	−0.695	−1.717
D	0.241	0.264
Sh	0.615	−0.264
R	−1.069	1.453
T	1.176	0.792
F	−1.256	−0.396

and their SD is 15. For example, if the SD of the sample is 3, then we can multiply each raw score by 5 and then the SD of these converted scores will be $5 \times 3 = 15$. Cronbach (1990) shows in detail how to convert scores in this way. Note that z-scores are a special case of standardized scores: z-scores are scores standardized on to a new mean of zero and a new SD of 1.

Tests that are interpreted in relation to the distribution of scores in a sample of typical subjects are called norm-referenced tests. In other words, the distribution of scores in the sample provides a frame of reference for interpreting the results. Scores are understood in terms of their relative standing.

The process of standardizing a test like an IQ test is called norming the test, and you will often see published norms for some test. The term norm used here comes from the word normative because norms tell you what subjects 'ought' to score. In other words, if your sample of subjects is similar to the sample used to norm the test, then your subjects' scores 'ought' to be distributed with the same mean and SD. When interpreting results from a standardized test like an IQ test, you need to satisfy yourself that the sample used to produce the norms provided with the test really is similar to your own subjects or clients. You also need to think carefully about the word 'ought'.

Converting scores fits in with the general idea that the investigator must seek useful descriptions of her data. Scores are converted in order to make their interpretation more straightforward, to reveal more clearly the important patterns in the data.

11.2   RELIABILITY

We turn now from the conversion of scores to assessing the reliability of the scores. It is one thing knowing that Harry's body image is nearly two SDs lower than the average of the sample on this occasion. It is another thing to infer that it would reliably turn out the same if we tested all the subjects tomorrow. Reliability is concerned with the consistency and the accuracy of the scores that a test produces. There are a number of formal statistical tests for reliability, which we survey next.

Let's start with the familiar equation:

M11.1: data = model + error

Translating this into the terminology of test scores:

M11.2: observed score = true score + error

The *observed score* is the score a subject actually got on some test. The *true score* is the hypothetical 'real' score of the subject. For example, Harry's body image observed score was 12. His true score is the score the test would give if it was providing a perfectly accurate measure of body image. This true score is said to be the average of an infinite number of measurements by parallel tests. For instance, the 'true' length of a given piece of wood is the average of an infinite number of measurements of the wood's length.

Reliability is, conceptually, the relationship between true scores and observed scores. If the test is perfectly reliable, then the true score and the observed score will be exactly the same. Typically, however, the observed score differs from the true score. The amount it differs by is a function of error variance. Thus, we can divide observed scores into two components. One part is attributed to the true value of the attribute we are trying to measure; the other part is attributed to error.

Error in psychological testing can arise in many ways. We should distinguish instrument error from pilot error. By instrument error, I mean problems with the test itself. For example, the questions used in a test of mechanical ability may not be directly measuring just 'true mechanical ability'. Scores may also be influenced by, for example, verbal intelligence or, notoriously, cultural familiarity with the content of problems presented in the test. If you are asked to work out whether an egg will smash when struck by an object weighing 200 g moving at 10 m/s, you may be assisted by intimacy with the anglo-saxon breakfast. By pilot error I mean the mistakes you make as tester and also extraneous influences on results introduced by the test situation. For example, you may influence results by the way you read out the test instructions to subjects. Or subjects' scores may be affected by room temperature, lack of sleep and any number of other variables which are unconnected with their mechanical skill. Both pilot error and instrument error reduce test reliability. In theory, reliability is the ratio of true score variance to observed score variance.

reliability = true score variance / (true score variance + error variance)

When there is no *error variance*, theoretical reliability is 1. Normally, however, reliability is less than perfect. We would like some way of working out what the reliability of a test is. The theoretical formula just given cannot be used in practice, of course, because we cannot discover the *'true-score variance'*. Therefore, alternative formulae have been put forward that allow us to estimate the reliability of a test. In general, these tests are based on the correlation coefficient. For example, reliability can be estimated as the correlation between scores you get from the test on Monday and scores you get from the same test on Friday. If the test is perfectly reliable, the scores will be exactly the same and so the correlation between Monday and Friday will be 1. The more unreliable the test, the greater the likely discrepancy between the two sets of scores and, therefore, the lower the correlation you'll get.

Generalizability theory actually examines error in terms of the different sources of the error. It focusses on sources of error that influence the interpretation of the test. For example, if we want to hire someone to do a mechanical job in an overheated garage, then error introduced by conducting the test in a stuffy room may not matter. Although we have not measured true mechanical aptitude, the discrepancy is not important because we do not need to generalize the result across other temperatures. On the other hand, if there is error introduced by the day of the week testing is done on, we do need to control that, because whoever is given the job has to work on each day. We do need to generalize the test score to other days of the week.

Generalizability theory involves building more explicit statistical models of observed variance. Rather than just using the straightforward model M11.3, you would use a model like M11.4.

M11.3: observed score = true score + error
M11.4: observed score = true score + day of week + error

This is exactly the same as introducing another explanatory variable in ANOVA. We are moving a source of variance out of general error variance and using it as an explicit term in the model. This allows you to be more precise in your analysis. The reliability tests we will look at now are, in a sense, less sophisticated than generalizability approaches. Nevertheless, they are sufficient for many purposes and are widely accepted.

11.2.1 Test–retest reliability

This approach simply correlates scores obtained on one occasion with scores (for the same subjects and the same test) obtained on another occasion. The reliability statistic is just the correlation coefficient. Test–retest reliability is often a function of time for psychological tests. The longer the gap between the first presentation and the second, the lower the reliability.

11.2.2 Parallel forms reliability

Scores obtained by two similar tests are correlated. The reliability of a test is its correlation with another test having similar content. Again, you can simply use the correlation coefficient. This method is suitable even if your test is a speed test in which subjects complete only as many of the items as they can. The crucial thing is to ensure that the parallel tests used really are parallel. That is, you need some criteria for establishing that the tests have similar content. One way this is done is by first establishing an item bank. Tests are then made up by randomly sampling a number of items from the bank. Tests composed by randomly sampling items from the same bank are then assumed to be parallel tests.

11.2.3 Split-half reliability

You can use this version even if you only have scores for your test from one set of subjects. The idea is to correlate one half of the test items with the other half. This test directly measures the internal consistency of the test. Typically, the scores for odd-numbered items are correlated with scores for even-numbered items. Split-half testing assumes that all the items on the test are measuring the same variable. It is not appropriate for tests that have subscales that measure a number of attributes.

The procedure involves calculating two scores for each subject in your sample. The first score is derived from only the odd items; the second from only the even ones. If you have n subjects, you end up with n 'odd' scores and n 'even' scores. These scores are then correlated.

In general, reliability tends to increase with the length of the test. The more items, the more reliable the test. The exception is when subjects are young children, for whom long tests are badly affected by fluctuations in attention. The split-half test estimates the reliability of half the test. The full test is, obviously, longer and therefore more reliable. A special formula, called the Spearman–Brown formula, is used to adjust the reliability estimate obtained from a split-half correlation.

$$r_{\text{test}} = (2 * r_{\text{half}})/(1 + r_{\text{half}})$$

In this formula, r_{test} is the reliability estimate for the complete test and r_{half} is the correlation between one half of the items and the other.

11.2.4 Item analysis

Individual questions on a test can be analysed in terms of their effectiveness. There are two main issues in item analysis, difficulty and discriminability.

The difficulty of an item is usually defined as the proportion of subjects taking the test who get the correct answer for that item. For example, if 10 subjects take a test, and eight get question 1 right, then the difficulty of question 1 is .8. If only three subjects get question 6 right, then the difficulty of question six is .3. On speed tests, where not all subjects even attempt some items, difficulty is defined as the proportion of subjects attempting the item who got it right. A good ability test will have items covering a range of levels of difficulty.

Item discrimination can be estimated by correlating scores that subjects got for a given item with their overall score for the test. Obviously enough, the better an item predicts the overall score of a test the more consistent it is with the aim of the test. In general, you just use the Pearson product–moment correlation to calculate this statistic. However, when the item scores are dichotomous, i.e. there are only two possible scores for each item, you do not call it the Pearson r. Instead it is known as the point-biserial correlation coefficient. There is a special formula for the point-biserial, related to the chi-square test, but it gives exactly the same numbers as Pearson's r. If both the item scores and the overall test results are dichotomous, you use a third statistic called the phi coefficient (pronounced to rhyme either with 'flea' or 'fly' depending who you listen to). The point-biserial, phi, and other special case correlation coefficients are discussed in detail in Siegel and Castellan (1988). Other techniques for item analysis are described in sources such as Ferguson (1981).

11.2.5 Intraclass correlation

This approach also examines internal consistency of tests. It makes use of the scores for individual items in the test. It checks that scores for all items are similar. In other words, a high intraclass correlation indicates high agreement among items. More specifically, a measure of this kind checks that the relative difficulty of items is the same across subjects. If a question is hard for the first subject, it should also be hard for the last subject. The intraclass correlation is often called the α-coefficient. A number of formulae can be used to calculate the α-coefficient for a test. Here is a version known as the Kuder–Richardson formula 20 (KR–20). This version is used when the test items are dichotomous.

$$r_{\text{test}} = \frac{k}{k-1}\left[1 - \frac{\Sigma pq}{s^2}\right]$$

where: k is the number of items on the test
     s^2 is the variance of the test
     p is the difficulty of an item
     $q = 1 - p$
and pq is summed across all items.

11.2.6 Standard error of measurement

Reliability coefficients are directly related to the confidence the tester can place in the accuracy of the scores produced. We say the true score is approximated by the observed test score. The greater the reliability of a test, the less error there is in the estimate it gives of true scores. The standard error of measurement (SEM) lets us place a precise confidence interval on test scores.

$$\text{SEM} = \text{SD} * \sqrt{1 - \text{reliability}}$$

where: SEM is the standard error of measurement

       SD is the standard deviation of the scores of a sample of subjects

       reliability is a reliability coefficient

For example, if we test a class of children and find the SD of their scores is 8, for a test with reliability 0.84, then the SEM is 3.2. This means that, if a given child's true score is 43, then 67 times out of 100 the test would estimate the score in the range 43 ± 3.2. The 95% confidence limits are given by doubling the SEM (43 ± 6.4).

We have seen above that scores can be interpreted in relation to a norm. Tests designed to be interpreted this way are said to be norm-referenced. Another way of interpreting scores is in terms of some external criterion. For example, a test of mental arithmetic might give results that let you conclude 'this person could work on a till' or 'this person could work in a stock exchange dealing room'. These interpretations refer to a task the subject can be predicted to be able to do. They do not refer to relative standing. Tests that should be interpreted in this way are said to be criterion-referenced.

A given test can often be interpreted as either criterion or norm-referenced from different points of view. For example, a law exam result might be interpreted either as a measure of the candidate's relative standing in the class or as an affirmation of the candidate's ability to practise in a given field of law.

11.3   VALIDITY

The validity of a test concerns the relationship between the test and inferences that are drawn from results obtained with the test. Cronbach (1990, p. 145) defines validity succinctly: 'Validation is inquiry into the soundness of the interpretations proposed for scores from a test.'

Suppose that you want to know how fast a particular car can go. There are a number of different tests that you could apply. First, you could simply time it over a fixed distance. That would be a direct measure of speed. Second, you could measure the power of the engine (in horsepower, say, or kilowatts). This would be quite a good measure, because, all things being equal, a car with a more powerful engine will go faster. However, it is not as direct a measure. The connection between power and speed is also influenced by the weight of the car and other features of its design. Therefore, conclusions about the relative speed of two cars based on a comparison of their engine power have less validity. Conclusions that rely on the power test will have to be more carefully qualified. A third test you could consider would be a test based on the colour of the car. Initially, this test does not seem to be a good test. There is no reason to expect colour to influence speed. However, one could argue that the colour test does have a little validity, albeit rather less than either of the other tests we have considered. Perhaps, for instance, drivers who like to drive at speed prefer certain colours. Perhaps manufacturers are aware of this and produce fast models in fast colours and slower cars in beige. If this is correct, then there will be a coarse relationship between the colour of a car and its top speed.

There is, then, a hierarchy of tests that can be used to compare car speeds. These tests vary in their validity and, consequently, in the extent to which conclusions based on them will have to be qualified. That is, there are more ways in which the inference from colour to speed can be undercut. In psychology the tests we use tend to be more similar to the colour test in terms of their validity. As psychologists we simply cannot lift the bonnet and measure the size of the engine. The phenomena we are interested in and try to explain are not amenable to direct observation.

A number of different kinds of validity are distinguished. The terminology used can vary from one author to another. However, I will briefly present a four-way classification.

11.3.1 Face validity

Face validity concerns whether a test, on the face of it, seems to be a good measure of the latent variable of interest. For example, the direct measurement of speed has good face validity. However, the colour test does not have a great deal of face validity. Another example of a test not having face validity is a question reportedly posed by a national rail company to potential employees. Applicants for work as cleaning staff were asked whether they would 'rather be a bishop or a colonel'. There is no obvious connection between the question and conclusions about the suitability of applicants.

11.3.2 Content validity

When a test has content validity, its items cover the domain of interest and are therefore appropriate. An examination whose questions cover the syllabus of the course has content validity. However, if a class on data analysis is examined by a question on the American Civil War, the test does not have content validity.

11.3.3 Construct validity

A construct is a mechanism that is believed to account for some aspect of behaviour. For example, working memory is a construct that it is believed can account for memory performance in many experimental settings. Or the trait introversion–extraversion is a construct hypothe-sized to account for a range of individual differences. To the extent that a test offers a direct measure of the mechanisms proposed in a theory, it has construct validity. For example, you might find that a test of children's spelling ability in their native language is correlated with their subsequent performance in a second language class. The spelling test will only have construct validity if you can explain how the ability it measures plays a causal role in second language learning. For example, you might hypothesize that spelling ability reflects a learning skill, or processing strategy, that is also needed in second language learning. If you can develop an account of the mechanisms underlying performance in the two tasks and show how they are linked, then you can give the test construct validity.

None of the three kinds of validity I have listed so far can be evaluated with a simple statistic. They must be evaluated by subjective judgement. However, the final kind of validity can be tested statistically.

11.3.4 Criterion validity

Criterion validity is related to the concept of criterion-referenced testing which we defined earlier. A test has high criterion validity if it correlates highly with some external benchmark. For example, if law exam results correlate highly with speed of promotion to the bench, then by that token they have high criterion validity. Similarly, even if you cannot endow the spelling test with construct validity, if it does successfully predict who will succeed in language classes, then it has criterion validity. Or if job applicants' preference to be bishops or colonels can predict who will be good at cleaning railway carriages, or perhaps even just stay longer in the job when hired, or show lower levels of absenteeism, then the question has criterion validity. In applied settings, criterion validity can be sufficient.

11.4   SUMMARY

The quality of inference you can make in any study depends on the quality of the measuring instruments you use. The quality of a measuring instrument has two main aspects: whether it measures what you want it to measure, validity; and whether it measures it accurately, reliability. You may also be concerned with the generalizability of measures you use.

12 RESEARCH PLANNING

Data analysis allows you to understand observations you have made. However, the process of setting up an investigation raises issues that influence the conclusions you can ultimately draw. To do good research, you need to find a topic that is interesting and you need to convert that interesting idea into a practicable study. The way you frame the study at the outset will largely determine whether the study can be useful. This chapter surveys some of the steps you need to take to get a project off the ground.

12.1 THE TOPIC

The most difficult part of carrying out a research project is identifying a good topic. It is best to select an area that you find personally interesting, for obvious reasons. For example, you might be especially interested in memory, or child development. However, you need to quickly focus on a specific research question. Ideas for more specific questions to address can come from a number of sources. It is sometimes a good idea to choose a topic that is related to the research interests of someone who could advise you, such as a member of staff in your department.

Another excellent idea is to look through the latest issues of psychology journals. There you may find articles describing research that interests you. Using a recent piece of research as a starting point is helpful in several ways. You start with an up to date view of what the key issues for research are. You can use the articles cited in the report as a starting point for your literature review. You may be able to use the same techniques for gathering data, and you may be able to follow the analysis of the results as an example for your own data analysis. Of course, you would not, in general, simply repeat the same study. Rather, you would extend it. You can build on previous work to extend it in a number of ways.

You can generalize a finding to a new group of subjects. For example, if a study has found that American college students consider swans and ducks more typical example of birds when they are pretending to be Chinese (Barsalou and Sewell, 1984), then you could try to see if the results are borne out for students in a different country. Or you could generalize the finding to a different task. Barsalou and Sewell used a method in which subjects listed examples. However, it is also known that the time it takes subjects to verify that an instance, such as a swan, is a member of a category, such as bird, is faster for more typical instances. You could investigate whether Barsalou and Sewell's conclusion that swans are considered more typical when students are pretending to be Chinese holds up when a different measure of typicality is used. Generalizing findings is a sensible way to develop a project. However, there is an even better way of starting from an existing piece of research and developing it. That is, try to think of an alternative explanation for the pattern of results that has been reported, and then design a study to test whether your alternative explanation can be refuted. This is more difficult to do.

When your project uses previous research in a direct way as a starting point, it can be useful to embed a partial replication of the original study in your project. For example, if you are trying to generalize the Barsalou and Sewell finding to verification time, you could also run a group of subjects using the exemplar listing method that they employed. This is useful because it checks the original finding, can check your own technique, and so rule out some possible explanations if you fail to generalize the result to the verification method. For example, if you fail to show that swans are verified more quickly when subjects pretend they are Chinese, there are several possible explanations. It could be that you ran the experiment badly and for that reason failed to show a difference. Or perhaps there was something different about your subjects that meant they did not respond to the instruction to pretend they were Chinese in the same way as Barsalou and Sewell's subjects. Indeed, any difference between your study and the original is confounded with the change in task.

However, if you also replicate the original study and you are able to repeat their findings when you run it the way the original investigators did, then you have evidence that incidental differences, such as different subjects or different experimenter, do not affect the results. This narrows the range of explanations for results in your new task and increases your confidence in your findings.

The process of refinement that takes a project from being an interesting idea and transforms it into a testable hypothesis, a design and a procedure, engages your psychological knowledge and skill to the full. To the extent that your project builds upon previous research, many aspects of this task are done for you. However, to the extent that you are breaking new ground, there are a number of issues that you will need to consider.

12.2 INTEGRATION WITH PREVIOUS LITERATURE

Good projects are usually closely linked to discussions of theoretical issues in existing studies. It is important to be able to show how your project is related to this earlier work and to show how it addresses theoretical questions raised there.

12.3 THE PRACTICAL HYPOTHESIS

The next step is to generate a specific and testable question, or hypothesis, that can be evaluated. Deciding whether your question is testable requires careful thought. For example, the question 'Are lawyers smarter than engineers?' is doubtless interesting. However, it needs to be refined considerably before it becomes a testable hypothesis. In particular, the word 'smart' needs to be defined. It is likely that different intellectual skills are needed for these professions. Engineers will be smart as engineers, lawyers as shysters. In the same way, it hardly makes sense to ask whether a weightlifter is as fit as a marathon runner. Each is fit for their specialization. You therefore need to be more specific. Does a weightlifter have as much endurance as a marathon runner? Does a lawyer perform better on analogical reasoning tasks than an engineer?

This example illustrates the way that constructs, such as intelligence, must be operationalized. Operationalization has two facets. First, you must devise a workable method for making measurements of the variable. Second, you must evaluate the relationship between this instrument and the psychological mechanisms you are using it to observe, which you believe underly and explain behaviour.

Finding a way to measure a variable involves identifying some feature of behaviour and recording it. You can record whether people make an error, how quickly they perform, which word they utter, how long a line they draw, which item they prefer, and so on. In every case, you select an aspect of behaviour that can be measured reliably. In addition, you choose measures which you believe reflect the construct you are interested in as directly as possible. For example, if you want to measure intelligence, you need to consider precisely what psychological mechanism you have in mind and how that is linked to behaviour on your chosen test. The issue here is construct validity, and addressing construct validity requires you to refine your picture of the underlying explanatory mechanism more precisely.

12.4   DIRECT AND INDIRECT, SUBJECTIVE AND OBJECTIVE MEASUREMENT

When you are devising or selecting instruments with which to gather data, it is useful to bear in mind two distinctions. First, as we saw in Chapter 11, instruments vary in the directness with which they measure an underlying variable. In psychological research, a degree of indirectness is inevitable because modern theories postulate intangible explanatory mechanisms. Nevertheless, some measurements are more direct than others. For example, a range of techniques has been used to examine the way people read sentences. One method is to record how long it takes subjects to read different kinds of sentence and to use differences in the time taken to draw conclusions about the processes involved. An alternative is to measure eye movements. Eye-tracking equipment can record which words the reader looks at, and how long they look at each word. This offers a more direct measurement of the time course of processing. However, it is important to emphasize that even a reliable record of eye movements is not a completely direct trace of the reading process. Furthermore, there may be a trade-off between the directness of a measurement and the difficulty of making it. In this example, for instance, both the equipment needed and the data gathered in eye-tracking studies are more complex.

Eye movement is an objective instrument. The movements actually occur in the world. No judgement or interpretation is needed to record their extent or duration. Indeed, they are recorded by apparatus. However, many psychological instruments are subjective. There are two ways they can be subjective. First, they can demand that the researcher makes a subjective judgement when they record the data. Second, they can require a subjective act from the research participant to generate the data. We will discuss each of these in turn.

Many kinds of data demand that the researcher subjectively judges some behaviour to record it. For example, if you were investigating the way interactions with their teachers differ between delinquent adolescents and other adolescents you might be interested to know whether delinquent adolescents are more aggressive towards their teachers. One way to investigate this would be to look at whether the delinquents more frequently make aggressive utterances. But to analyse the conversations, you will have to classify some utterances as aggressive, and that is inevitably a subjective judgement. This kind of subjectivity is common in psychological research, especially in social psychology. A researcher investigating infant communication might look at the intonation contours of mother and child to see whether they are congruent. Many investigators will judge the intonation contour subjectively. Another study might be interested in differences in the degree to which parents control their children as they prepare to cross a road. This, too, is potentially a highly subjective judgement.

Subjectivity in the process of recording data should be minimized wherever possible. There are six steps that you can take to achieve this. First, an objective measurement can sometimes be substituted for a subjective judgement. For example, instead of judging intonation, you could analyse samples of speech using software that tracks changes in pitch. Pitch change is closely linked to intonation patterns. Second, the scope of judgements can be reduced and broken down into smaller, less subjective, judgements. For example, rather than making a single overall judgement about the degree of control a parent has, control could be operationalized as a series of behaviours (does the parent speak to the child? does the parent hold out their hand to the child?). The data recorded is then more objective and more easily verified by a third party. Third, the researcher making the judgement should, ideally, not know the 'correct' answer. For example, if the principal investigator who designed the study predicting that delinquents would be more aggressive also judges the utterances, knowing which were said by delinquents, there is an obvious risk that their judgements will be biased. Where possible, then, the person classifying data should not be familiar with or have a stake in the hypothesis driving the investigation and, at the very least, should be unaware which condition each piece of data is derived from. Fourth, the researcher who makes the record should be carefully instructed or trained so that they understand the criteria for making judgements. For example, if you make judgements about intonation contours, you should be trained to do this. The judgements of trained observers are likely to be more reliable. Fifth, the reliability of judgements should be checked. This can be done by comparing judgements with those of another judge. Statistical techniques for evaluating this comparison were discussed in Chapter 11. Finally, subjectivity in recording data can be minimized by repeating measurements. For example, even writing down a time from a stopwatch requires you to judge where the hands are pointing. By recording the mean of several repeated timings, the error can be minimized. If errors introduced by subjectivity are random, then repetition will tend to cancel these errors out.

It is important to note that there is a range of degrees of subjectivity. The greater the subjectivity of an instrument, the more important it is to take the steps outlined. For example, the subjectivity involved in transcribing a conversation (producing a written record of what was said by each participant) is not a great as the subjectivity involved in then coding the utterances in terms of a participant's intention or motivation in making each utterance. The potential for subjectivity to vitiate a study is greater the more subjective the instrument is.

The second way a psychological instrument can be subjective is that it may require the participant to reflect upon or judge their own psychological processes. At one extreme lies the introspective method in which the participant is invited to directly report their own thoughts. This method was developed and refined exquisitely in the early days of experimental psychology, but fell into disrepute. Investigators found that different subjects, reflecting on similar psychological events, made conflicting reports. There was no way to detemine which report was correct. The dissatisfaction with introspective methods directly contributed to the rise of behaviourism in psychology. Behaviourism insists that only observable, objective, data may be used and only observables may find a role as constructs in a psychological theory.

Modern psychology, however, tends to permit subjects' judgements to play a role as data. Sometimes, this subjectivity is theoretically inherent. That is, it is necessary theoretically to have the subject reflect on their knowledge and tell you what they are aware of. In other cases, the reason for using subjects' judgements is pragmatic: it is a practical way to gather data.

An example of an inherently subjective variable is found in studies of explicit memory. Theorists now draw a distinction between implicit and explicit memory. Explicit memory requires that the subject is aware of remembering. This can be tested by asking whether they recall some fact. For example, do you remember what you had for breakfast yesterday morning? When you answer a recall question, you are reporting your own awareness of your mental state. However, even when people cannot recall a fact, it can sometimes be shown that they have some memory for it. For example, subjects might first be shown a list of words. You can test their memory by asking them to recall the words. However, you could also ask them simply to identify the words in a task where each word is presented briefly. Words from the list will tend to be primed and so responses to those words are faster. The priming effect suggests that there is a residual memory for having seen the word in the list. This implicit memory can be observed even when the subject no longer explicitly remembers the word. Evidence that amnesic patients, who perform poorly on explicit memory tasks, performed around the same level as normal subjects on implicit memory tasks has helped to focus attention on this important distinction. It is inherent in the theoretical understanding of the distinction that tests of explicit memory require a subjective judgement by the participant.

Participant judgements are also used for pragmatic reasons. For example, when studying the way people solve problems, Newell and Simon (1972) have used think-aloud data. In a think-aloud study, subjects literally are instructed to think out loud. A typical problem involves solving a puzzle. What the subject says is transcribed and annotated to identify steps in their reasoning process. This method provides a practical way to gather information about the way subjects approach the task of solving such problems. Questionnaires also make use of participant judgements. The subject responds to items on the questionnaire by reporting information about themselves or their beliefs. This information can be relatively objective (e.g. how old are you?), but often is quite subjective (e.g. do you think politicians are more honest than journalists?).

Where participant subjectivity arises, four key issues should be addressed. First, the reliability of the instrument should be assessed with regard to the consistency of its measurements. This was discussed in Chapter 11.

Second, the results should be compared where possible with results obtained by another instrument, ideally one that has a distinct rationale. For example, in studying a reasoning task which requires subjects to select from a set of four cards, Evans has used both think-aloud data (which cards do they mention?) and eye-movement data (which do they look at longest?) to address the question of how participants select cards. Where data from distinct instruments is consistent in the conclusions it points to, evidence is said to converge, and convergent evidence can be relatively convincing.

Where each of the instruments being compared has a distinct rationale, the basis for accepting each as a valid instrument is different. For example, eye-movement data is justified by an argument that people look at the things they pay attention to and so by measuring what they look at the longest, you obtain an index of the focus of their thought. For think-aloud data, the rationale is that there is a good, if pehaps coarse, correspondence between conscious awareness and psychological focus. If people tell you what they are aware of, that is a guide to the course of processing. The more distinct the rationale for two instruments, the more independent will be the report each gives. Just as a court is more likely to be satisfied when it has more than one independent witness, so converging evidence from distinct instruments is persuasive to psychologists.

Thirdly, it is possible that the act of making the observation may alter psychological events. For example, perhaps the strategies subjects use to solve problems when they must think aloud are different from those they otherwise use. Whether this occurs can be tested. You first establish some other criterion for describing peformance. In problem solving, this might be which problems they find hardest or which kinds of error are most frequent. You can then compare the peformance of subjects asked to think aloud with a control group who are given the same problems but do not have to think aloud. If the groups differed in that they found different problems hard or made different kinds of mistake, then that would be evidence that the think-aloud version of the task did influence the way problems were tackled. This kind of investigation has been carried out for the think-aloud method. Ericsson and Simon (1980) report that subjects who were asked simply to think aloud showed similar peformance to a control group. However, they found that when subjects were additionally asked to justify their thoughts (e.g. why are you considering the blue card?), they showed changed patterns of respond-ing. The additional step of considering why they were thinking what they were did seem to influence what they thought.

Finally, it is important to consider what the relationship is between the report a subject gives and the underlying psychological reality. It is a trueism of modern psychology that people do not have transparent, direct access to their own thought processes. It is less clear what mechanisms link cognition to subjective experience. The interpretation of data which involves participant subjectivity is qualified by this link. Where a variable is inherently subjective, such as recall in the context of the distinction between explicit and implicit memory, the link becomes the very object of theorizing.

The process of operationalizing variables lies at the heart of the planning of your project. It is important to consider both the reliability and validity of your instruments. These issues can be approached by considering how directly your instruments measure the underlying psychological constructs and whether the instruments depend on sub-jective judgement.

12.5   DESIGN

There are different type of research project, and these can be roughly ordered in terms of the kinds of inference they can allow you to draw. Four will be described here.

- experimental
- quasi-experiments
- observational studies
- correlational studies

12.5.1 Experimental

The ideal study is an experimental study. It is ideal in the sense that it provides a model to which other kinds of study can be related. It also allows the strongest conclusions to be drawn. There are three key features of an experiment in psychology: the experimenter manipulates at least one variable; the experimenter chooses the levels of manipulated variables; subjects are assigned to groups randomly. In addition, a good experiment seeks to refute a hypothesis which has been derived from a precise theoretical account of some phenomenon. This provides a co-herent explanatory framework, which is usually necessary for results to gain acceptance in the scientific community. The three key features enable an experimenter to draw conclusions about a causal relationship between the variables that are manipulated and the outcome for each subject. To demonstrate a causal effect it is necessary, although not sufficient, to show that there is a contingency between cause and effect. Whenever the cause is present, the effect occurs. The manipulation of a variable allows the experimenter to vary the presence of the cause. In some studies, the contrast will simply be whether the hypothesized cause is introduced or removed. For example, one group of children is shown a television programme portraying violence, another group is not shown the programme. In many studies, however, the degree to which the causal variable is present is varied. For example, in Hicks' choice reaction time study, described in Chapter 2, the number of choices was varied across a range. In such cases, when a relationship is causal, the experimenter anticipates that the degree to which a cause occurs is related to the degree to which an effect is present. The third feature is necessary to eliminate alternative explanations for any link found between the manipulated variable and the outcome. For example, if it was found that children who saw the television programme portraying violence subsequently showed a greater preference for 'violent' toys (toy guns, say), then there would be two possible explanations for this difference between the groups. It could be attributed either to the causal effect of watching the programme or to a difference between the groups which existed before they watched the programme. For example, perhaps one group contained a set of friends who happened to have been playing a game of cowboys just before the experiment started. The purpose of random assignment is to neutralize any such differences between the groups. If participants are assigned to groups randomly, then, in the long run, there should be the same number of cowboys in each group. Random assignment provides a guarantee that if the experiment was repeated many times, the groups will be equal on every variable other than the variable the experimenter has manipulated. This licences the conclusion that any difference observed in the outcome can be attributed to the manipulation. Random assignment is important.

12.5.2 Quasi-experiment

A quasi-experiment is just like an experiment, except that at least one of the independent variables is not manipulated by the experimenter and subjects are not assigned randomly to groups (Cook and Campbell, 1979). Instead, naturally occurring groups of subjects or levels of the variable are used. For example, a quasi-experiment might divide children into groups on the basis of their school class. Let's say that one class is given a classical Piagetian number conservation task. They are shown two rows of counters and have to confirm that their equality persists even when the counters in one of the rows are spread apart. The other class is given the 'naughty teddy' version of the task (McGarrigle and Donaldson, 1974). A toy bear scatters the counters, and their manipulation is presented to the child as incidental. If the children in the class who see the counters scattered by the naughty teddy are more successful, what can you attribute this difference to? The obvious explanation is the difference between the tasks. However, because children are not randomly assigned to groups, there may be other systematic differences that could explain the finding. For example, one class might be slightly older having joined the school as a group when they reached the age for admission, or one class might have recently covered a relevant topic with their teacher. In a quasi-experiment, the conclusions drawn need to be qualified more carefully.

Quasi-experiments are unavoidable in certain areas of psychology. For example, if you study the relationship between socio-economic status and skill at piano playing, you will be unlikely to persuade a research council to give you a grant to randomly assign participants to different income groups. Besides, it would not be very nice to assign any subjects to an extremely high income condition — they would hate it. The natural formation of the groups you study may also be intrinsic to the investigation. For example, if you want to compare relationships in teenage gangs to relationships among office workers of the same age, setting up the groups by random assignment would interfere with the processes that create the differences in relationships that you want to observe. The relationships are forged in the process of group formation. Indeed, to some extent one might argue that group formation is a key constituent of the relationships. To randomly assign subjects, student volunteers perhaps, to gang membership or office work would be to interfere with the phenomenon you are investigating. And so, although an experiment is an ideal, in many situations a quasi-experiment is as good as it gets. The quasi-experiment is preferred for practical reasons, for ethical reasons, or for reasons of ecological validity.

12.5.3 Observational studies

Observational studies involve simply watching and recording behaviour. Where experiments set up contrasts from which inferences can be deduced, an observational study amasses a collection of observations in the hope that generalizations can be made inductively. A purely observational study is conducted without preconceptions about which kinds of behaviour are important. All behaviour is recorded and this database of observations is then trawled for consistent patterns. For example, you might observe a parent playing with his or her child and record each time either smiles. You then notice that smiling tends to be coincidental:

parent and child smile together. This pattern repeated over several instances leads you to hypothesize that parents and children show affective congruence. The observational work leads you to a hypothesis that you can subsequently test. As an exercise, you might think about what would be needed to make the affective congruence idea a testable hypothesis.

In reality, purely observational work as I have described it does not exist. Every psychologist has certain preconceptions about behaviour and mental life. At the very least, you have views about which behaviours are interesting. Some psychologists are drawn to language, some to gestures. These preconceptions focus and bias your observations. This is not only inevitable, it is essential. Any real-life event, such as a conversation, is rich in detail and it is not practicable to record every detail. For example, if you transcribe a conversation (i.e. record it in written form), you can simply record the words that are said. Or you can record the intonation, the pauses, details of the accents of the speakers, accompanying gestures, eye movements, changes in posture or breathing patterns, and so on. To record the words alone takes a great deal of time. To try to record everything would be rather costly. The observer inevitably selects features for recording, and features that get recorded systematically are invariably chosen because the investigator expects them to be interesting.

Frequently observational research proceeds through the gradual development of a way to describe the kind of event being studied. This language of description is evolved in steps, each step being prompted by a hypothesis, or hunch, about which aspects of behaviour are related to the phenomenon the psychologist wants to study. For example, the social psychologists Bull and Mayer (1993) studied the peformance of politicians in television interviews. They observed real interviews that took place in the run up to a General Election in the United Kingdom. They recorded features of the conversation such as whether the politician answered questions directly or instead equivocated. They applied the concept of 'face' to this data. The concept of face derives from the work of Goffman and corresponds roughly to the everyday concepts of dignity, honour or reputation. Bull and Mayer evolved the hypothesis that skilled politicians are more likely to equivocate when they are asked 'no-win' questions in which any direct answer they gave would mean a loss of face. For example, the interviewer Robin Day asked Neil Kinnock whether trade unions would have their position restored if his party won the election. To answer yes or no would offend a proportion of those he would hope might vote for him. An equivocal answer would not be great, but it would make the best of a bad job. Bull and Mayer found that by this index, John Major, then the leader of the Conservative Party, was a more skilful interviewee than Neil Kinnock, who led the Labour Party.

12.5.4 Correlational studies

Correlational studies produce the weakest inferences of the four kinds of study I have described. In a correlational study, you merely examine associations between variables. For example, you might investigate whether participants who smoke more cigarettes tend to drink more coffee. If you find there is a positive relationship, it is an interesting observation, but the result leaves open many possible explanations. You can say little about whether smoking itself causes greater coffee drinking or vice versa. Or alternatively, whether some other variable that you may not have even observed, such as extraversion, leads to both more smoking and coffee drinking.

The four kinds of study outlined, experiments, quasi-experiments, observational studies and correlational studies, provide a framework that you can compare your project to. When you plan your project, consider carefully whether your design enables you to draw the inference you want to draw.

There is one more distinction among kinds of study that is worth mentioning. The pilot study plays an important role in preparing the ground for an investigation. It can be used to test whether the apparatus works, whether the instructions can be understood by subjects, and so on. This can be done using just one or two participants. A pilot study can also be used in the very early stages of investigation to evaluate which features or variables play an important role. An exploratory study is set up with low power and with less concern than usual for issues such as balancing sample size across cells. The intention is to identify variables which are important and which can be included in a more carefully designed study at a later time. This allows a rapid and cheap initial survey of the empirical terrain.

12.6 SAMPLE SIZE

The number of subjects you need to run depends on a number of variables. If you know, or can estimate, certain quantities, such as the size of the effect you will find, then the number of subjects you should run can be worked out using a statistical formula. I will outline this procedure shortly. However, there are a couple of quicker, rather rough and ready, ways to establish a sample size which you may find it more practical to rely on.

The easiest way is to follow the example of previous research. If you are using a previous study as the basis for your own project, then this is the obvious approach to use. Simply sample about the same number of subjects as the previous study. For this approach to be valid, you must follow a previous study which did establish a statistically significant effect. The previous study should also use a fairly similar task, a similar testing instrument, have about the same degree of difficulty for subjects, and should have employed participants much like the ones you plan to recruit.

The second method is even cruder, and has no statistical validity, but is widely used. Use about 24–60 subjects, with at least 16 in each group if you use a between-groups design. The more time you have been allocated for the project, the nearer the top of the range the number of subjects should be. The shorter the time it takes to test each subject, the more subjects you should test. If you take very few data points from each subject (less than five, say), then double the number of subjects tested. This method merely satisfies a pragmatic criterion: when a psychologist reads your project their impression is likely to be that you have run enough subjects. Sadly, that is often good enough.

The third rough and ready method is to follow guidelines suggested by statisticians. Statisticians occasionally suggest minimum numbers of subjects that should be run before certain kinds of analysis are appropriate. Table 12.1 gives a few examples. Bear in mind that these are generally minimum numbers to get the statistic off the ground. They do not guarantee that you will have enough data to detect effects even if they are present. Nevertheless, they provide a broad guide.

There are a number of parameters of a study that influence how many subjects are needed. In statistical theory, the concept of power is used when calculating the number of subjects needed. The power of a statistical test is the probability that it will detect a true effect if that effect is present. The parameters that influence the number of subjects you need are the parameters that determine power. The better the power of your test, the fewer subjects you need to detect an effect. Relevant

Table 12.1 Textbook advice on sample size

Test	Minimum number	Good number	Reference
Chi-square	5 per cell (estimated)	—	Widespread
Log-linear analysis	5 per cell (estimated)	—	Bakeman and Robinson (1994)
Correlation	28	783	Cohen (1992)
Multiple regression	5 per predictor	20 per predictor	Tabachnik and Fidell (1989)
Stepwise regression		40 per predictor	Tabachnik and Fidell (1989)
Two-sample t-test	49 total sample	126–784	Howell (1992)
Analysis of variance	16 per group	80–400	Bratcher et al (1970)
Factor analysis	5 per observed variable	50 poor; 200 fair; 1000 excellent	Comrey (1973)

parameters are listed in the following table, which you can use as a broad guideline. In the next section, we will see how these parameters can be used to calculate the number of subjects needed with precision.

1. The size of effect you expect to find. The larger the effect, the fewer subjects you will need.
2. The reliability of the instrument. The more reliable the instrument, the fewer subjects you need.
3. The variance of the measurement. The greater the variance, the more subjects you need.
4. The α-level chosen for statistical significance. Stringent α-levels that set a high hurdle for significance reduce the power of your test.

In addition, the power of the test you run is affected by the choice of statistic (e.g. *t*-test versus Mann–Whitney U) and is affected by the nature of any violations of the assumptions of that statistic by your data. For example, if your data satisfy the assumptions of the *t*-test, then the *t*-test is more powerful. However, the Mann–Whitney U is more powerful when its assumptions are satisfied but assumptions of the *t*-test are violated by the data. Interestingly, the power of the Mann–Whitney U turns out to be exactly the same in all circumstances as the power of a *t*-test performed on any data set which has been rank-transformed.

You can influence the number of subjects you need in a number of ways. The number can be reduced if you:

● accept a less strict α-level;
● use more reliable instruments;
● reduce error variance by exercising better experimental control;
● choose one statistic rather than another to make the test;
● avoid violations of assumptions (e.g. non-linear relationships in correlation or multiple regression reduce power).

I will illustrate one way to calculate the number of subjects needed. It requires you to supply an estimate of the effect size you expect to find and an estimate of variance.

12.6.1 Effect size

Size of effect can be described as the number of units difference you expect to find in your contrast per SD unit. That is:

effect size $= M_1 - M_2/\text{SD}$

For example, if you expect the mean of the first group to be 3 units greater than the second group using an instrument with an SD of 8, then:

$$d = 3/8 = 0.375$$

When you have more than two levels, then the difference in means is the largest difference you expect to find. That is the difference between the mean for the highest scoring group and the lowest scoring group. Note also that the sign of the difference is ignored. Other measures of effect size can be used, but for present purposes d is convenient.

The smaller the effect size you want to detect, the harder it will be and the more subjects you will need to establish that the effect is significant. Note that you need to supply estimates for the means of both groups and for the SD. You just have to make a judgement of what these are likely to be. However, previous studies on the same topic can serve as a guide.

Once d has been calculated in this way, the sample size needed for a given level of power can be read off from tables provided originally by Bratcher *et al* (1970). The number of subjects needed per group for power set at .5 is reproduced in Table 12.2, and gives the numbers of subjects required in a between-groups ANOVA. It is useful to remember the rule of thumb, derived from the tables, that with 16 subjects per group or fewer you have a better than 50/50 chance of detecting any true difference between mean scores only if the difference is at least one SD in magnitude. To get the numbers required for power of .8, roughly double the number of subjects indicated in Table 12.2. For power of .95, treble it.

Remember that if you do find a significant difference, then by definition you ran enough subjects. If, however, after running the study you find there is no significant difference, then statistical power is a key consideration when interpreting your finding. For example, say you run an experiment in which you record the mean time it takes subjects to

Table 12.2 Minimum number of subjects in each group to achieve power = 0.5, adapted from Maxwell and Delaney (1990). Original source Bratcher *et al* (1970).

Number of levels	d				
	0.25	0.5	0.75	1.00	1.50
2	124	32	15	9	5
3	160	41	19	11	6
4	186	48	22	13	7
5	207	53	24	14	7
6	225	57	25	15	8

decide whether a string of letters is a word of English. This time is termed lexical decision time and is known to be sensitive to a number of variables such as the frequency of the word: more common words produce faster decisions. In this study, however, you are interested in examining the effect of ink colour. One group of subjects will see words printed in red ink. A second group sees the words printed in blue ink. Perhaps, you hypothesize, words printed in a more familiar ink colour will produce faster decisions. (In fact, you would probably use a re-peated measures design for a study like this, but developing the design thoroughly would take us too far from the point.) You randomly assign 16 subjects to each group. However, when you run the experiment, you find that the difference between the groups is not significant at the .05 α-level. Imagine that the result is that the mean for red is 536 ms, the mean for blue is 586 ms, and the (pooled) SD is 75. What can you conclude?

The most straightforward conclusion would be to reject your experi-mental hypothesis and report that ink colour makes no difference to lexical decision. However, there are two important alternative explanations.

First, establish what the power was for this design. For these data, you should be able to easily check that d can be estimated at 0.67. From Table 12.2, you can see that with 16 subjects per group and an effect of this magnitude, the power is about .5. That means that if there really was a difference, you only had a 50/50 chance of finding it significant. There-fore, one reason why you did not obtain a significant difference may be just that your design lacked power. You ran too few subjects.

Before you reject any hypothesis on the basis of a non-significant result, do check the power that was available. If you are drawing conclusions on the basis of the absence of a difference, another approach is to slacken the α-level. For example, if the difference obtained is not significant at the $\alpha = .2$ level, then you can be more confident that there really is no difference. In other words, set the criterion for declaring no difference high if you want to claim that the absence of a significant difference implies that there is no true difference.

The second alternative explanation is that the instrument you used was not sufficiently sensitive to detect the difference. For example, perhaps the difference is greater for less common words, but for high frequency words lexical decision is so fast that ink colour has only a minor influence. If you included only high frequency words in the list, then you may have encountered a ceiling effect. If so, with rare words, the difference might have been more noticeable. Poor sensitivity is an especially plausible explanation for the lack of a significant difference where you have created a new instrument. For example, you may have devised your own questionnaire. The less reliable the instrument, the harder it is to detect effects.

12.6.2 Exceptions

There are some exceptions to the guidelines on sample size just described. The number of subjects is an issue for psychologists mainly because it is costly to obtain data from a subject. It take time and effort, and sometimes money.

One exception is survey or census data. Such data is obtained by circulating a questionnaire to participants, and is relatively cheap to obtain in the sense that you do not have to be present yourself when the questionnaire is filled in. Indeed, you may be in the happy position of being able to address the questions that interest you using data that someone else has gathered. For example, the Economic and Social Research Council keeps an archive of data gathered in studies it has funded. In situations like this, it should be easier to obtain a large sample. Indeed for surveys you will be more concerned to have a sample that is representative of the population you want to generalize to. For example, if you survey people to canvas their voting intentions, you need a sample that is representative of the electorate. The proportion of old and young people surveyed should correspond to their proportions in the population, and so on for other characteristics that might be related to voting behaviour such as income. Stratified random sampling involves randomly selecting participants from each group in the population that you want to represent. Many opinion poll companies use a slightly different technique called quota sampling, which is quicker and easier. With quota sampling, you randomly sample respondents from the population. As each respondent is recorded, the subgroup they come from is identified. Each subgroup has a quota: a target number of respondents. As each respondent is recorded, they are checked off against the quota for their subgroup. The difficulty with quota sampling is that it is biased against a particular type of subject. Potential respondents who are hard to contact will be unlikely to appear in a quota sample. Being hard to contact is related to other characteristics which may be relevant to a survey.

The other striking exception is the single case study. In neuropsychology or psychiatry, studies frequently report data from just one subject who displays an unusual pattern of behaviour. For example, the patient H.M. displayed a distinctive pattern of memory loss. He underwent surgery which removed parts of his temporal lobes and hipocampus to control epilepsy. He was subsequently able to remember events which occurred before the operation, but unable to remember episodes which occurred afterwards (Milner, 1966). New information could not be stored. In studies of this type, the qualitative pattern of behaviour displayed by the subject is the important observation. A range of tests is usually carried out and the subject's peformance can be reported in comparison to the range of performance found in the general population.

For example, you might report that the subject's verbal IQ was normal, but report standard scores for other tasks where extreme performance was observed.

12.7   ETHICS

In psychological investigations, subjects are people. It is important to treat these people in an appropriate way. This is the first ethical consideration in psychology. The Golden Rule is to do unto others as you would have them do unto you. That is, imagine yourself as a participant in the study and imagine how you would feel. This is a good start, but it is not always sufficient (Mackie, 1977). You need to take into account that the participants in your study may have different values from you and may feel differently about different kinds of event. An obvious example is that an older person may be less tolerant of discomfort than you. People who differ from you in race, religion, gender, culture or belief may not be prepared to accept things that you would tolerate. You have to imagine that you are in their place, with their beliefs, undergoing the conditions of the study. How would they feel?

It is rather easy to assume that because a procedure would be acceptable to you, no-one else would mind. It can be hard to appreciate the objections of other people, particularly if they differ from you in background or experience. You therefore should consider discussing proposed procedures with members of the population you wish to study. For example, if you plan to secretly video the interactions among people in a prison visiting room, you might assume that because they are being watched and supervised anyway, your observation should not disturb them. However, this conclusion might very well be incorrect. Perhaps prisoners and their visitors give privacy greater weight than you imagine. Before going ahead, discuss this with people who have been prisoners or who have visited prisoners to gauge how they view it. People who are like your intended subjects can provide you with a more accurate perspective on what is acceptable.

Because it is not always easy to place yourself in the position of another, and in order to avoid uncertainty about the ethical obligations that psychologists have, ethical codes have been devised by psychological associations. You should get a copy of the relevant code from your national psychological association. These codes cover a whole range of activities in detail and indicate the standards required. Rather than repeat the codes at length, I will draw out three key themes.

12.7.1 Deception

First, you must be honest with participants. You must not conceal things from them or tell them things which are untrue. Before they agree to participate, you must explain in straightforward and clear terms what is involved. This includes explaining that they may withdraw from the study at any point without losing out in any material way (they will still be paid or receive course credit where applicable, for example). However, it is often useful to deceive participants in your study so that they do not fully realize what you are trying to find out. Although you might prefer to not deceive subjects, there are several practical reasons why you will often do it.

We saw earlier that peformance could be influenced by certain kinds of instruction to reflect on performance. Participants who have to explain their thoughts as they think aloud show different patterns of behaviour. The possibility that certain kinds of observation may influence performance should be considered even in studies that use objective measurements. If participants realize they are being observed, they may behave differently. For example, if you studied the relationship between academic performance and the number of visits students make to the college library, telling subjects about your study in advance might affect their reading behaviour.

It can also be important to withold information from your co-workers. In particular, as we saw earlier, researchers involved in classifying or coding behaviour should not know which classication of a particular behaviour will support the hypothesis being tested. There is otherwise a risk that their classification will be biased. Again, having researchers work blind can be important even where the instrument is relatively objective. Rosenthal conducted a study in which different research assistants were given different accounts of the purpose of a study. They were then told to test a number of subjects on behalf of the principal investigator. The data they brought back consistently favoured the hypothesis they thought they had been detailed to test.

Sometimes you need to conceal the precise nature of the task from subjects. For example, participants who are told when they first hear a voice that they will be asked to identify the voice later have approximately a 0.6 chance of correctly identifying it a day later. However, correctly recognizing a voice is often important in legal cases where, at the time of an incident, the witness did not realize they would need to remember it. For example, someone may pretend to be an employee of a utility company, such as an electricity company, to gain entry to a house. Only later, the occupant realizes that property was taken during the visit. It is important to know whether people are likely to make correct identifications in such circumstances. To study this experimentally, Clifford and Flemming (unpublished study, reported in Clifford, 1983) constructed a situation in which subjects were not told that their memory would be tested. An experimenter entered a bank and engaged a clerk in a brief conversation. The first experimenter left, and another researcher went in to the bank to ask the clerk to identify the voice from a set of tapes. Although clerks were correct 41% of the time if they were tested immediately after the initial conversation, their chance of correctly identifying the first experimenter's voice after only four hours' delay was 0.04. It clearly makes a substantial difference to accuracy that the bank clerks did not realize that their memory for the voice would be tested.

In many situations, then, psychologists accept that they may have to deceive their participants. The important thing is to minimize deception, never to use it as a way of collecting data you expect the participant would not give you permission to gather, explain clearly to participants at the end of the study what was going on and offer to not use the data if they would prefer that it was not used.

12.7.2 Protecting participants from harm

It is obviously important that your participants are not damaged. For example, testing people's reactions by firing darts at them at varying speeds is not on. However, participation in psychology experiments carries the risk of other kinds of harm or upset. For example, you might be interested in whether mood affects performance on certain tasks. You design a study in which one group of participants is induced to feel a bit sad and their performance is compared to a control group. Mood induction can be achieved, for example, by asking subjects to read through a list of depressing words several times. This will probably effect a small change in affect for most people, and at the end of the task they can read a list of cheerful words to jolly them up again. However, for certain kinds of people, such a those who are already clinically depressed, this procedure could be harmful. It would be advisable, then, to screen participants for clinical illness before carrying out the procedure. You could do this simply by asking a question like 'Are you seeing a doctor or anyone like that because you have been feeling unhappy or isolated?' There are obvious limitations to a simple screening question, and if you are concerned you could consider using a formal diagnostic tool such as Beck's Depression Inventory as a screening measure.

12.7.3 Confidentiality

What you learn about individual participants in the course of your study is confidential. Normally their data will be reported anonymously, and often it will be aggregated with data from other participants in the same group. You do not discuss information about individuals with anyone. However juicy the news that Betty's friend Samantha Tiggywinkle was awful on the vocabulary test, do not share it.

12.7.4 Problems

In any arena, ethical guidelines sometimes fail to clarify the best course of action. This can happen because different guidelines appear to conflict. For example, if you screen for depression and find a person who appears to be clinically depressed but who is not receiving treatment, what do you do? You will want to put them in contact with some agency, but it would be a breach of confidentiality to telephone the health centre and say 'John Smith needs help because he's mad.' Indeed, you may not be confident in your diagnosis. Here confidentiality conflicts with the desire to put this person in touch with support. Because you cannot be sure of your diagnosis and you are an experimentalist rather than a clinician, you should be equally wary of saying to the participant 'John, you're off your head, see a doctor.'

I will not attempt to resolve this dilemma here. If you are uncertain what to do, consult a psychologist who has relevant experience. This could be your project supervisor, for example. Most psychology departments will have an ethics committee which you can approach for advice. If, when you are planning your project, you anticipate difficulties or you are unclear whether the study is ethical, you can submit your proposal to the ethics committee for consideration. In some settings, for example if you are working with patients, you will be obliged to have your study approved by an ethics committee in advance.

To conclude this discussion of ethics, consider whether the following studies would be ethically acceptable.

You are interested in where people choose to sit in the library in relation to other readers. You sit in the library surreptitiously observing where people sit. You record your observations in a notebook.

Most psychologists would regard this as ethically acceptable. Although you have not obtained consent or even debriefed subjects, you have recorded behaviour which occurred in a public place and the tenor of behaviour is not particularly intimate.

You are interested in the way parents and children interact when they cross roads. You invite parents to bring their children to your laboratory. As they arrive, you secretly film them crossing the road.

This would still be acceptable to most psychologists again because this is a public place and the behaviour recorded is not exceptionable. However, you should explain to both the parent and the child what you have done as soon as possible and obtain consent from the parent and, insofar as they can give it, from the child too. If they object, you should delete the tape without viewing it. The persistent record on tape raises issues of confidentiality. You should not keep the tape after the end of the study without permission from the participants, it should only be put to uses the participants have consented to (e.g. do not sell it to TV shows) and their anonymity should be protected.

You are studying the relationship between the speed at which people read text and their understanding of the content. You give subjects tests of reading speed and of text comprehension.

This is a straightforward study that raises no great ethical difficulties. However, you should be careful to debrief participants in a way that dispels any sense they may have that they performed badly. Often participants view psychological tests like exams and are keen to get a good score. Reassure them that the task is not an ability test and that they are not in competition with other participants.

You are studying the circumstances in which bystanders are prepared to become involved in a dramatic event. You have an accomplice, or stooge, pretend to steal a bottle of ketchup from a grocery store. You stand nearby and note whether bystanders intervene as they make good their escape.

This study raises many issues and should probably be scrutinized by your local ethics committee. Obviously, for example, the owner of the shop must consent to you doing this, and you really ought to give the sauce back. However, the key point to draw from this case is the effect it may have on bystanders. Vulnerable people find crime terrifying, and may suffer long-lasting effects if they witness a dramatic event like this. Although the shop is a public place, it would be important to ensure you debriefed any bystander. Your debriefing should include providing a way for them to contact you, or your institution, if they subsequently have concerns.

12.8 SUMMARY

Psychology is great, because you can design studies to find out interesting things about people. Few sciences provide students with this kind of creative opportunity. However, you need to take care to set up the project well so that it is possible to draw relevant conclusions. You must also take care of the participants in your project.

REFERENCES

Ableson, R. P. 1995: *Statistics as principled argument*. Hillsdale, N.J.: Lawrence Erlbaum Associates.

Andrews, D. F. (1972): Plots of high-dimensional data. *Biometrics* **28**, 125–36.

Baddeley, A. 1993: Working memory or working attention? In Baddeley, A. and Weiskrantz, L. (eds), *Attention: Selection, Awareness and Control*. Oxford: Clarendon Press, 152–70.

Bakeman, R. and Robinson, B. F. 1994: *Understanding log-linear analysis with ILOG: An interactive approach*. Hillsdale, NJ: Lawrence Erlbaum Associates.

Barsalou, L. W. and Sewell, D. R. 1984: *Constructing representations of categories from different points of view*. (Technical Report No. 2) Atlanta, GA: Emory University, Emory Cognition Project.

Bratcher, T. L., Moran, M. A. and Zimmer, W. J. 1970: Tables of sample sizes in the analysis of variance. *Journal of Quality Technology* **2**, 391–401.

Brewer, W. F. 1988: Memory for randomly sampled autobiographical events. In Neisser, U. and Winograd, E. (eds), *Remembering Reconsidered: Ecological and Traditional Approaches to the Study of Memory*. Cambridge: Cambridge University Press, 21–90.

Broadbent, D. E. 1971: *Decision and stress*. London: Academic Press.

Broadbent, D. E. 1979: Human performance in noise. In Harris, C. (ed.), *Handbook of Noise Control*. New York: McGraw-Hill.

Bull, P. and Mayer, K. 1993: How not to answer questions in interviews. *Political Psychology*, **14**, 651–66.

Chernoff, H. 1973: Using faces to represent points in K-dimensional space graphically. *Journal of the American Statistical Association*, **68**, 361–368.

Clifford, B. R. 1983: Memory for voices: The feasibility and quality of earwitness evidence. In Lloyd-Bostock, S. M. A. and Clifford, B. R. (eds), *Evaluating Witness Evidence*. Chichester: John Wiley and Sons.

Cohen, J. A. 1992: A power primer. *Psychological Bulletin*, **112**, 155–59.

Comrey, A. L. 1973: *A First Course in Factor Analysis*. New York: Academic Press.

Cook, T. D. and Campbell, D. T. (1979): *Quasi-experimentation: Design and analysis issues for field settings*. Boston: Houghton Mifflin.

Cronbach, L. J. 1990: *Essentials of psychological testing*. New York: Harper and Row.

de Groot, A. D. 1965: *Thought and choice in chess*. The Hague: Mouton.

du Toit, S. H. C., Steyn, A. G. W. and Stumpf, R. H. 1986: *Graphical exploratory data analysis*. New York: Springer-Verlag.

Duncan, J. 1993: Selection of input and goal in the control of behaviour. In Baddeley, A. and Weiskrantz, L. (eds), *Attention: Selection, Awareness and Control*. Oxford: Clarendon Press, 53–71.

Ericsson, K. and Simon, H. 1980: Verbal reports as data. *Psychological Review*, **87**, 215–51.

Estes, W. K. 1991: *Statistical models in behavioural research*. Hillsdale, NJ: Lawrence Erlbaum Associates.

Everitt, B. and Hay, D. 1992: *Talking about statistics: A psychologist's guide to design and analysis*. London: Edward Arnold.

Everitt, B. S. 1978: *Graphical techniques for multivariate data*. London: Heinemann Educational Books.

Ferguson, G. A. 1981: *Statistical analysis in psychology and education*. New York: McGraw-Hill.

Hicks, W. G. 1952: On the rate of gain of information. *Quarterly Journal of Experimental Psychology*, **4**, 11–26.

Hill, M. 1990: *Data analysis with Systat: An introductory handbook*. Evanston, Ill: Systat Inc.

Hirst, D. 1983: Structures and categories in prosodic representations. In Cutler, A. and Ladd, D. R. (eds), *Prosody: Models and Measurements*. Berlin: Springer-Verlag, 93–109.

Howell, D. C. 1992: *Statistical methods for psychology* (3rd ed.). Boston: PWS-Kent Publishing Company.

Kline, P. 1994: *An easy guide to factor analysis*. London: Routledge.

Mackie, J. L. 1977: *Ethics: Inventing right and wrong*. Harmondsworth: Penguin.

Maxwell, S. E. and Delaney, H. D. 1990. *Designing experiments and analyzing data*. Belmont, CA: Wadsworth.

Maxwell, S. E., Delaney, H. D. and Dill, C. A. 1984: Another look at ANCOVA versus blocking. *Psychological Bulletin*, **95**, 136–147.

McGarrigle, J. and Donaldson, M. 1974: Conservation accidents. *Cognition*, **3**, 341–50.

Milner, B. 1966. Amnesia following operation on the temporal lobes. In Whitty, C. W. M. and Zangwill, O. L. (eds), *Amnesia*. London: Butterworths, 109–33.

Myers, J. L. and Well, A. D. 1991: *Research design and statistical analysis*. New York: HarperCollins.

Newell, A. and Simon, H. 1972: *Human problem solving*. Englewood Cliffs, NJ: Prentice-Hall.

Rosenthal, R. and Rosnow, R. L. 1985: *Contrast analysis: Focused comparisons in the analysis of variance*. Cambridge: Cambridge University Press.

Sauerwein, H. C., Nolin, P. and Lassonde, M. 1994: Cognitive functioning in callosal agenesis. In Lassonde, M. and Jeeves, M. A. (eds), *Callosal Agenesis*. New York: Plenum Press, 221–33.

Schachter, S., Goldman, R. and Gordon, R. 1968: Effects of fear, food deprivation, and obesity on eating. *Journal of Personality and Social Psychology,* **10,** 91–7.

Schunn, C. D. and Vera, A. H. 1995: Causality and the categorisation of objects and events. *Thinking and Reasoning*, **1**(3), 237–84.

Siegel, S. and Castellan, N. J. 1988: *Non-parametric statistics for the behavioural sciences*. New York: McGraw-Hill.

Sternberg, S. 1969: Memory scanning: Mental processes revealed by reaction time experiments. *American Scientist*, **57,** 421–57.

Tabachnik, B. G. and Fidell, L. S. 1989: *Using multivariate statistics*. New York: Harper and Row.

Toothaker, L. E. 1991: *Multiple comparisons for researchers*. Newbury Park, CA: Sage.

Tukey, J. W. 1977: *Exploratory data analysis*. Reading, MA: Addison Wesley.

Warrington, E. K. and Weiskrantz, L. 1970: Amnesic Syndrome: Consolidation or retrieval? *Nature*, **228,** 628–30.

Waxman, S. R. and Hatch, T. 1992: Beyond the basics: preschool children label objects flexibly at multiple hierarchical levels. *Journal of Child Language*, **19**(1), 153–66.

Wilkinson, L. 1986: *Systat: The system for statistics*. Evanston, Ill: Systat Inc.

Winer, B. J. 1971: *Statistical principles in experimental design* (2nd ed.). New York: McGraw-Hill.

INDEX